Managing a Special Needs Trust

A Guide for Trustees

Managing a Special Needs Trust

A Guide for Trustees

Barbara D. Jackins, Esq.

Richard S. Blank, Esq.

Ken W. Shulman, Esq.

Harret H. Onello, Esq.

Managing a Special Needs Trust:
A Guide for Trustees

This book is intended to provide accurate information on the topics of government benefits and special needs trusts. However, the rules, regulations, and laws covering these areas change frequently. The materials may become outdated. Neither the authors nor the publisher are providing any legal services by selling this book. A reader who requires legal services should consult with a qualified attorney who specializes in providing the kinds of legal services the person requires.

DisABILITIESBOOKS, Inc.
33 Pond Ave. #919
Brookline, MA 02445
phone: 617-879-0397
www.DisABILITIESBOOKS.com

ISBN: 0-9845852-4-9

Printed in the United States of America

Acknowledgments

This book would not have been possible without the support and encouragement of many friends and colleagues. We thank Hyman G. Darling, Esq., of Springfield, Massachusetts, for his capable assistance with the tax sections. Linda L. Landry, Esq., and Barbara L. Siegel, Esq. of the Disability Law Center in Boston, Massachusetts, assisted with the public benefits and housing materials. Janet Lowder, Esq. of Cleveland, Ohio, served as a critical reader for this book and made many helpful suggestions. We also thank our clients and readers for their kind words and encouragement over the years.

About the Authors

Barbara D. Jackins practices law in Belmont, Massachusetts. Her practice centers on areas of the law that affect people with disabilities and their families, such as estate planning, Medicaid planning, SSI and other public benefits, guardianship, and trust administration. She has served on the Governor's Commission on Mental Retardation Task Force on Public-Private Partnerships. Barbara currently serves on the Board of Directors of the NWW Committee (Newton, MA), an agency that provides community housing for people with disabilities. She is a member of the National Academy of Elder Law Attorneys and a 1978 graduate of Suffolk University Law School. Barbara is the author of *Legal Planning for Special Needs in Massachusetts: A Family Guide to SSI, Guardianship and Estate Planning* (AuthorHouse, 2010).

Richard S. Blank is a member of the firm Rubin and Rudman LLP in Boston, Massachusetts, where he practices in the areas of trust administration and estate planning (http://www.rubinrudman.com). He has extensive experience drafting and administering special needs trusts and preserving government benefits. A substantial part of his practice is focused on integrating personal injury settlements into special needs trusts and then administering those trusts. He is a 1987 graduate of Georgetown University Law Center.

Harriet H. Onello practices elder law and family law in Lexington, Massachusetts. She is the author of a chapter on Planning for Incapacity in a three-volume book entitled *Estate Planning for the Aged or Incapacitated Client in Massachusetts*, published by Massachusetts Continuing Legal Education, Inc. She participates as faculty for continuing legal education programs and has made a number of community presentations on elder law issues. She received an M.Ed. from Harvard Graduate School of Education and a J.D. from Suffolk University. Harriet is a founding member and a Past President of the Massachusetts Chapter of the National Academy of Elder Law Attorneys.

About the Authors

Ken W. Shulman is a partner at Day Pitney LLP in Boston, Massachusetts (http://www.daypitney.com). His general estate planning practice includes estate planning and related issues for elders and for families who have children with disabilities. He is a former Director of the Massachusetts Chapter of the National Academy of Elder Law Attorneys and is a member of the Special Needs Alliance. Past and current board memberships include the Asperger's Association of New England, the Combined Jewish Philanthropies Committee on Disabilities and The Arc of Greater Boston. Ken has written and lectured extensively on special needs estate planning and preserving eligibility for government benefits for elderly clients and clients with disabilities. He is a graduate of Northwestern University and the Boston University School of Law.

Table of Contents

Appendices

Introduction

This is the third edition of our book on special needs trusts. The former name was *Special Needs Trust Administration Manual: A Guide for Trustees*. The first edition was written in 2004 because we noticed that many trustees — although well-intentioned — did not know how to properly manage a special needs trust. Some trustees were afraid to spend any money for fear of getting into trouble with the government. Other trustees were spending the trust funds in ways that needlessly reduced the beneficiary's public assistance. The benefits of the trust were being lost.

It doesn't have to be that way. It is true that managing a special needs trust can be challenging. But if you are diligent and take the time to learn the rules, you can avoid most pitfalls. You might even find that managing a special needs trust can be a rewarding experience. You have the opportunity to do a lot of good for someone.

We — the authors — are all attorneys with many years of experience writing and managing special needs trusts. We wrote this book for professional trustees as well as for people who have taken on a special needs trust to help a friend or relative with a disability. In short, this book is for anyone who is managing — or considering managing — a special needs trust.

In this book, we will tell you how to:

- Understand the rules of major public benefit programs that provide cash, medical care, and housing assistance to people with disabilities.

- Use practical strategies to pay for items and services the beneficiary needs, without reducing public benefits.

- Set up a budget, keep accurate records, and open a trust checking account.

- Properly invest the trust funds.

- Periodically account to the beneficiary for what you have done with the money.

- Deal with the state Medicaid agency that might receive the remaining trust funds when the beneficiary dies and the trust ends.

- Pay federal, state, and local income taxes on the trust earnings.

Readers of the previous editions will notice one major change. While the earlier editions focused almost exclusively on Massachusetts laws and procedures, this book applies to all states. We don't mean to suggest that we cover every rule in every state. If we did, this book would have taken years to complete, and you would probably not be able to lift it. Instead, we cover uniform statutes that have been adopted in most states. We also focus on the rules of major federal benefit programs that provide cash, medical benefits, and housing subsidies to people with disabilities.

Let us also tell you what this book is not. Although we have tried to make this book reasonably complete, we cannot possibly address every situation that might come up. Instead, we have drawn on our collective experience to describe common scenarios you might encounter and suggest how to handle them.

This book is not a substitute for working with a qualified attorney in your state. Keep in mind that most public benefit programs — although federal in origin — are managed at the state and local levels. The rules can vary from state to state. It is essential to work with an attorney in your state who can guide you through the local practices.

Last, managing a special needs trust is not a "do it yourself" project. Although trustees bring many different skills to the role, few of us can do everything on our own. In addition to an attorney, a financial adviser, tax professional, social worker, or case manager may be able to assist you. Make the most of these people's expertise. They can save you time and money. Most importantly, they can help you be an effective trustee and enrich the beneficiary's life. In the end, that is what the special needs trust was intended to accomplish.

Most government programs that assist people with disabilities have been created by federal law and implemented by detailed federal and state regulations. This book contains many references to those laws and regulations. The legal references are primarily for attorneys. However, they may also interest lay readers who want to know more about the laws that govern special needs trusts.

The enabling statute for the Supplemental Security Income (SSI) program is located at section 42 of the United States Code (U.S.C.) §1381[1], et seq.[2] The regulations that govern that program can be found in section 20 of the Code of Federal Regulations (C.F.R.) §§ 416.101 – 416.2227.

The enabling statute for the Social Security Disability Insurance (SSDI) program is located at 42 U.S.C. §402, et seq. The federal rules that govern that program can be found at 20 C.F.R. §§404.1 - 404.2127.

The enabling statute for the Medicaid program is 42 U.S.C. §1396, et seq. Program rules are also located at 42 C.F.R. 400, et seq.

The POMS (Program Operations Manual System) are volumes of guidelines that interpret Social Security laws. These guidelines are relied on by workers at the Social Security local district offices. The POMS, which can provide a wealth of specific examples to guide the trustee, can be found on the Social Security Administration website, http://www.ssa.gov.

The federal housing program standards discussed in this book, established by the Department of Housing and Urban Development (HUD), are located at 24 C.F.R. §5.609. They can be accessed online at http://www.gpoaccess.gov.

---

[1] The symbol "§" stands for section. The symbol "§§" stands for more than one section.

[2] The term "et seq." means "and the following ones."

Chapter I
The Special Needs Trust

This book will tell you how to properly manage a special needs trust. But before reading about the specifics, it helps to understand some basics — what a special needs trust is, the different kinds of trusts, and the role of public benefits. This chapter explains the basics.

What is a Special Needs Trust?

A special needs trust starts with a written agreement between the person who creates the trust (the *grantor*) and one or more trustees. The trustee uses the funds for a *beneficiary* with a disability according to the instructions in the trust document.[3] Most trust documents specify that the funds will be used to pay for items related to the beneficiary's "special needs" and other items the government does not pay for or sufficiently cover.

A special needs trust can assure that a person's funds will be properly managed. The trustee *must* account to the beneficiary for what he or she has done with the funds. If there is no trust, a person (such as a sibling) may be holding funds for a person with a disability with only a vague understanding about what he or she is supposed to do with them. The funds could be mismanaged or even lost altogether. A trust can prevent the funds from being misused.

Another benefit is continued access to government assistance. This is important because many people with disabilities rely on government programs to provide them with items like cash, food, housing, staff supervision, day programs, employment support, transportation, and medical care. However, in order to qualify for most government benefit programs, a person can only have limited income and few resources. If a person has too much income or too many resources, he or she cannot qualify.

[3] Throughout this book, the term "beneficiary" will mean the person with a disability who receives benefits from the special needs trust.

While government programs are essential, they just cover the basics. They do not provide everything a person needs to have a good quality of life.

This is where the special needs trust comes in. The funds in a properly drafted and managed special needs trust are not counted toward the resource limits for most government benefit programs. As a result, a person can have a trust fund and still qualify for most government assistance. The funds can pay for some goods and services that government benefits do not provide. These can include vacations, clothes, recreation, and special therapies. In this way, the beneficiary's quality of life can be enriched.

What happens to any money that may be left in the trust when the beneficiary passes on? In some cases, the funds must be applied to the person's Medicaid bill.[4] In other cases, the remaining property can be distributed to one or more *remainder beneficiaries* that were named when the trust was created. The remainder beneficiaries may be individuals or charitable organizations. As we explain later in this chapter, whether or not the Medicaid program must be reimbursed usually depends on the source of the funds that were placed in the trust.

The Trustee's Role

The trustee's role is to manage the trust. You must carefully follow the instructions in the trust document. You also have duties that may not be outlined or described anywhere in the written document. Throughout this book, we describe your duties.

What are your basic responsibilities? For one thing, you must protect the trust property and make sure that it is not lost or misused. You also need to properly invest the trust assets so they earn a reasonable rate of return.

You are also responsible for deciding how the trust funds will be

[4] The Medicaid program provides comprehensive medical benefits to individuals who are poor or have disabilities. Medicaid is funded by the state and federal governments and managed by the states. The Medicaid rules vary from state to state. The Medicaid program is explained in detail in Chapter 4, "SSDI, Medicare, and Medicaid."

spent. Most special needs trusts use the term *sole discretion*. This means that only you, the trustee, can decide how the trust funds will be used.

Another responsibility is to make sure that any required taxes are paid. Some special needs trusts pay taxes on the income they earn from investments, while others "pass through" the income to the beneficiary. In either case, it is your responsibility to report the income to the federal and state governments. Tax reporting is explained in more detail in Chapter 11, "Taxes."

You are also responsible to account to the beneficiary (or the beneficiary's legal representative) for how you are handling the trust. Most trusts (including special needs trusts) require the trustee to provide annual financial accounts to the beneficiary. These accounts must show the income received, the expenses paid, and how the assets are invested. The accounting requirements are explained in Chapter 10, "Everyday Management."

The Two Kinds of Special Needs Trusts

The funds in a special needs trust can come from different sources. Sometimes the trust is created by the beneficiary himself or herself. This is called a *first party trust*. (A first party trust is also called a *self-funded* or *self-settled trust*.) Another kind of trust is created by a third party (that is, someone other than the beneficiary). This is called a *third party trust*. Either of these trusts can be a so-called payback trust (described later in this chapter).

For purposes of management, the differences between the two kinds of trusts are not all that significant. The same basic rules will apply regardless of the source of the funds. However, to be an effective trustee, it is important to understand which kind of trust you are managing.

First Party Trust

A *first party trust* contains property that originally belonged to the beneficiary before it was put in the trust. The property could include an inheritance, gift, proceeds of a personal injury lawsuit, or other property already owned by the beneficiary.

The motive to create a self-funded special needs trust is often public benefits. Many people with disabilities need assistance from public benefits at one time or another. Many public assistance programs have strict asset limits. For example, a person cannot receive SSI benefits (discussed later in this chapter) if he or she has more than $2,000 in resources. This is also true for the Medicaid program in many states.

A person who wants to qualify for these programs and has excess resources can transfer them to a self-funded special needs trust and obtain benefits right away. In order for the government to approve the special needs trust, it must:

- Be irrevocable. This means that the person cannot change his or her mind and get the money back.

- Be created by the person's parent, grandparent, or legal guardian, or by a court. This means that the person's parent, grandparent, or legal guardian must sign the trust document that establishes the trust. If none of these relatives are available and the person does not have (or need) a legal guardian, a court must create the trust. Due to a wrinkle in the Social Security and Medicaid laws, the person cannot create his or her own trust.

- Benefit only the person with a disability. The person's parents, siblings, spouse, children, or other family members may not receive benefits. (However, these persons may benefit from the trust after the beneficiary with a disability has died.)

- Provide that when the beneficiary dies, any remaining trust funds will be used to reimburse the state for the Medicaid benefits the beneficiary received while he or she was alive.[5]

[5] These requirements are for special needs trust created on or after January 1, 2000 for a person who wants to qualify for SSI. There are different rules for trusts created before that date. The Medicaid programs in some states may also have different requirements. A trust that requires the state to be paid back for the beneficiary's Medicaid expenses can be known by different names — a payback trust, OBRA '93 trust, or d(4)(A) trust. All these references are to 42 U.S.C. 1396p(d)(4)(A), which is part of the Omnibus Budget Reconciliation Act of 1993 that authorizes that kind of trust.

If the person does not want (or need) public benefits, the trust does not have to be so restrictive. The person can sign the trust document that establishes the special needs trust. There is no need for a family member, guardian, or court to be involved (see the second bullet point). Also, the state Medicaid office does not need to be paid back when the beneficiary dies and the trust ends (fourth bullet point).The remaining funds can pass to the *remainder beneficiaries* the person named when he or she created the trust. These could be family members, friends, or charitable organizations.

Third Party Trust

A *third party trust* contains assets that originally belonged to someone other than the beneficiary before they were placed in the trust.[6] Someone such as a parent or grandparent (a third party) gives his or her property to a trust for a beneficiary with a disability, such as a child or grandchild. The property can be transferred during the person's lifetime or at death under a will, life insurance policy, retirement account, or other arrangement. In many cases, the trust is *revocable* while the grantor is alive. This will permit the grantor to change the trust if his or her circumstances change. On the grantor's death, however, the trust becomes *irrevocable*, and no changes can be made.

What happens to any funds that may be left in a third party trust when the trust ends because the beneficiary has died? In most cases, the funds should pass to the remainder beneficiaries the grantor named when he or she created the trust. Alternatively, the beneficiary may be permitted to write a will and specify who will receive the funds. This is called a power of appointment. The important point here is that *any remaining funds do not have to be applied to the beneficiary's Medicaid bill.*

There is one situation when a thirty party trust must provide for Medicaid reimbursement. That is when the grantor needs to qualify for public benefits himself or herself. A common situation involves a parent who needs nursing home care but cannot qualify for public payment because he or she has too many resources. (The resource limit in 2010 for nursing home-level Medicaid benefits is $2,000 for a single person.)

[6] A third party special needs trust may also be called a supplemental needs trust. However, we do not use that term in this book.

In that case, the parent can transfer the excess resources to a third party trust for a son or daughter with a disability. The parent can qualify for Medicaid benefits immediately, without incurring a waiting period. (In most cases, a person who transfers resources to a trust must wait five years to get benefits. However, the five-year rule does not apply if the beneficiary is under age 65 and permanently and totally disabled, and the trust provides for government reimbursement.) The trust will benefit the son or daughter, not the parent. When the son or daughter dies, any remaining funds will be applied to the child's — not the parent's — Medicaid bill.

Public Benefits and the Special Needs Trust

One of the trustee's jobs is to spend the trust funds. You can spend them on fun things like a winter vacation, line dancing lessons, or new clothes. Or you can pay for not-so-fun things like medical equipment or dental care. Or mundane items like the gas or electric bill. The point is, you are supposed to use the funds for the beneficiary and not just allow them to accumulate year after year in the trust.

Sometimes how you spend the trust funds can affect the beneficiary's public assistance. The Supplemental Security Income (SSI) program is a case in point. SSI pays a monthly cash benefit to its participants. However, the financial rules are strict. If a recipient receives more than $20 in cash in any month, the SSI benefit will be reduced on a dollar for dollar basis. If you give the beneficiary too much cash in any month, he or she could lose the entire SSI benefit for that month. These rules are explained in Chapter 3, "SSI."

But what if you pay the beneficiary's bills instead of giving him or her cash? In some cases, the SSI benefit could still be reduced. Under the SSI rules, if a third party, including a special needs trust, pays for any food or housing items for an SSI recipient that cost more than $20 per month, the SSI benefit will be reduced for that month. Fortunately, the reduction cannot exceed about one-third of the monthly benefit. (In 2010, the maximum reduction is $244 per month.) This is explained in more detail in Chapter 3, "SSI."

How can you best use the trust funds so that the beneficiary's public benefits will not be reduced or eliminated? Throughout this book, we give you advice and strategies for dealing with this challenging situation. If the beneficiary receives SSI, we advise you to:

- Avoid giving any cash directly to the beneficiary.
- Pay the beneficiary's bills instead of giving money to the beneficiary.
- Avoid paying the beneficiary's housing and food related expenses, if that is possible.

If the beneficiary does not receive SSI, you do not have to be so vigilant. For example, Social Security Disability Insurance (SSDI) recipients can get unlimited assistance from a special needs trust and not incur a reduction in benefits. The SSDI program rules are explained in detail in Chapter 4, "SSDI, Medicare, and Medicaid."

Government "Payback" and the Special Needs Trust

Some parents of children with disabilities erroneously believe that any money left in the special needs trust when the child is gone must be paid over to the government. Since most parents prefer that the money go to other family members, they are reluctant to use a special needs trust. They may omit the child from their estate plan, or they might leave the child's money to a relative and hope for the best.

This is unfortunate, because these parents are missing a significant planning opportunity. A special needs trust can be an effective way to manage money for a person with a disability. The person can receive valuable public assistance and still have a source of funds to pay for items that public benefits do not cover. Moreover, parents' concerns about paying the government are misplaced. In most cases, a special needs trust that contains a parent's funds is not required to pay back money to the government.

It is true that *some* special needs trusts require some of the money to go to the government when the trust ends. The most common situation is the one we described earlier in this chapter where a person wants to obtain SSI benefits but has too much money. The person can put the money in a special needs trust and qualify immediately for SSI. When the person dies and trust ends, the remaining trust funds must be used to repay the government for the person's Medicaid benefits.

There is only one instance when a *relative's* money in a special needs trust must be used to pay the government. That is the situation we described involving an elderly, sick parent of a son or daughter with a disability. Rather than spend the few remaining dollars on nursing home care, the parent puts them in a special needs trust for the son or daughter. The parent can obtain nursing-home level Medicaid benefits immediately, and the son or daughter can receive lifetime benefits from the trust. But when the son or daughter dies and the trust ends, the state must be reimbursed for the son's or daughter's Medicaid expenses from any remaining trust funds.

Except for this limited situation, the funds that parents contribute can stay in the family. This is also true for a special needs trust created by a grandparent or other relative. When the family member with a disability passes on, the remaining funds can go to other relatives who were named to receive them when the trust was established.

Trust Terms	
Account	A summary of the trust's financial activity for a specific period of time, usually a year.
Corpus	The property that makes up the trust. This could be bank accounts, bonds, mutual funds, real estate, life insurance, or other kinds of property.
Distribution	A payment from the trust. When the trustee spends the trust funds, he or she makes a distribution.
Grantor	The person who creates the trust. The grantor is sometimes called the donor, settler, creator, declarant, or trustor.
Lifetime beneficiary	The person who receives benefits from the trust while he or she is alive. (In this book, we refer to the lifetime beneficiary as "the beneficiary.")
Payback trust	A trust whose assets must be used to reimburse the state for the beneficiary's Medicaid costs when the beneficiary dies. Also called an "OBRA '93 trust" or a "d(4)(A) trust."
Remainder beneficiary	The person(s) or organization(s) that will receive the property that is left in the trust when the trust ends upon the beneficiary's death.

Chapter 2
Getting Started

In this chapter, we've compiled a list of items to get you started. Note that not all these items apply to every situation. Some of them only pertain to opening a new trust. Others only apply if you are taking over a trust that is already up and running. By following these recommendations, you will be able to take control of the trust assets and use them for the beneficiary.

Read the Trust Document

In order to properly manage the trust, you must understand its terms. Unfortunately, most special needs trusts have a lot of confusing jargon and complicated legal terms. Still, you can't be sure what you are supposed to do until you become familiar with the trust document. Here is a strategy we suggest:

- Make a copy of the trust document to use as a work copy.

- Read the document from the beginning to the end, highlighting the important information like the names of the trustee, the successor trustees, and the people or organizations that will receive any property left in the trust when the beneficiary dies. Also note whether the trust terms prohibit you from spending the funds on any particular items.

- Write down anything you don't understand.

- Set-up a meeting with an attorney to answer your questions. The attorney's role is discussed later in this chapter.

Meet the Grantor

If the grantor (the person who created the trust) is still living, meet with him or her. Find out what motivated the grantor to create the trust and how he or she wants the funds to be used.

Often parents who create special needs trusts have strong preferences about how the trust funds should be used — yet these preferences may not be described anywhere in the trust document. For example, a parent might want the trust to pay for an annual vacation for a son or daughter. Or the parent might prefer that a son or daughter live in the family home with a paid staff person. Unless you ask the grantor, you might not know these preferences. If the grantor is not living, other family members might have insights that will help you learn his or her intent. Besides family members, there might be other sources of information about the grantor's wishes. Sometimes, parents (or others) have written a "side letter" or a "letter of intent." Such informal documents can give valuable personal instructions to the trustee.

Meet the Beneficiary

If you do not already know the beneficiary, spend some time with the person. Find out what he or she is like. If the beneficiary cannot communicate effectively, find out who represents his or her interests. This could be a legal guardian, advocate, agent under a power of attorney, family member, or someone else involved with the person's care.

You should find out how much assistance the beneficiary will need from the trust. Thus, you will need to speak to the beneficiary and other individuals who are familiar with his or her needs. You should also find out what resources, including government benefits, are available to meet the beneficiary's needs.

If you are taking over from a prior trustee, find out if the distributions the person made were adequate. Were there any needs that were not met? If so, see if you can increase the amount of distributions.

Find out which Public Benefit Programs Assist the Beneficiary

Many people with disabilities receive some kind of public assistance. They might get SSI, SSDI, Medicaid, and/or a housing subsidy. But as we explain throughout this book, sometimes when you spend money from the trust, the beneficiary's public assistance could be reduced or even eliminated. For example, if you give a person who receives SSI more than $20 in cash in any month, SSI will be reduced on a dollar for dollar basis. Thus, you should avoid giving a person who receives SSI any cash. If the beneficiary has a federal housing subsidy like Section 8, any recurring payments you make from the trust (like monthly cell phone bills or utility charges) could be considered income that increase his or her rent. (This is explained in detail in Chapter 7, "Housing.") Therefore, before you spend any money from the trust, it is important to find out which public benefit programs assist the beneficiary and what the pertinent rules are.

Obtain an Employee Identification Number

If the trust does not already have an Employer Identification Number (EIN), you must obtain one from the Internal Revenue Service.[7] The EIN should be used on all trust bank accounts and investment accounts. Do not use your own Social Security Number or the beneficiary's Social Security Number. Detailed instructions on how to obtain an EIN are located in Chapter 11, "Taxes."

Choose a Qualified Attorney

In order to properly manage a special needs trust, you will need the assistance of an attorney who has experience working with special needs trusts and public benefits. The attorney has several important functions.

[7] An EIN is the trust equivalent of a person's Social Security Number. The term "employer" does not mean that you will be employing anyone.

An attorney can:

- Tell you how to use the trust funds in ways that will not disrupt the flow of public benefits.

- Explain your fiduciary duties. (A fiduciary is a person who holds a position of trust and responsibility. A trustee is a fiduciary for the beneficiary.) While every state has its own rules that govern fiduciary activities, these rules are not usually described anywhere in the trust document. Such rules may prohibit the trustee from doing things like borrowing money from the trust, loaning money to the trust, and combining the trust property with his or her own assets. The attorney can explain the fiduciary rules in your state.

- Assist you with any conflicts of interest that might come up. For example, let's say the beneficiary — a child who has received funds from a personal injury lawsuit — needs adequate housing and transportation (such as an adapted van), which you are able to purchase with the trust funds. However, other family members — parents and siblings — will also likely benefit from these purchases How do you maintain your loyalty to the child beneficiary? An attorney can help you sort through these thorny issues.

- Put you in touch with other professionals who can assist you, such as a tax professional to prepare and file the annual income tax returns, or a financial adviser to assist with investments. Information on how to locate qualified professionals is located in Chapter 14, "Getting Help."

Review a Schedule of the Trust Assets

To effectively manage the trust, you will need to identify the property that makes up the trust. The property could include items like bank accounts, mutual funds, real estate, and life insurance. The grantor, his or her adviser, or the prior trustee can provide you with a list. (However, if you are opening a new trust, see the next section of this chapter.) Make sure that each item is properly registered in the name of the trust and uses the trust's Employer Identification Number. If the trust owns a life insurance policy, retirement asset, or annuity, make sure you have a current schedule of beneficiaries.

Transfer the Assets to the Trust

If you are opening a new trust, you must register the property in the name of the trust. It isn't enough that the grantor *intended* that the property would belong to the trust. You must take specific steps to register it. The particular steps will depend on the kind of property that will make up the trust.

- Bank accounts. Any bank accounts must be titled in the name of the trust. For example, the name on the bank account might be "John Jones, Trustee of the Jack Jones Special Needs Trust."

- Real estate. If there is any real estate, a deed that names the trust as the owner must be recorded at the local registry of deeds.

- Stocks, bonds, and mutual funds. These kinds of assets must be registered in the name of the trust.

- Life insurance policies. If the trust has been named as the beneficiary of a life insurance policy, you will need to collect the benefits. To do so, you must complete the necessary paperwork and provide it to the insurance company.

- Retirement accounts. If the trust is the beneficiary of a retirement account, you must contact the plan administrator to arrange to collect the benefits. You should discuss the different distribution options with the plan administrator or your financial adviser (or both). The trust might be able to stretch out the distributions over the beneficiary's lifetime, thereby reducing income taxes.

Accept the Trusteeship

If you did not sign the trust document when the trust was created, you should formally accept the trustee position. You do this by signing a form called an Acceptance. (The Acceptance form is discussed in Chapter 8, "The Trustee.") Then notify anyone who is holding trust assets (banks, investment companies, etc.) that you are the trustee. This will allow you to receive the bank statements and deal with the trust property. If you are taking over from a former trustee, have the person sign a Resignation form. Trustee resignations are also discussed in Chapter 8, "The Trustee."

Review Insurance Coverages

If the trust owns any property that should be insured, such as real estate, motor vehicles, valuable artwork, etc., you should make sure there is adequate coverage for the property. A trustee has a duty to protect the trust property against the risk of loss. If the beneficiary rents an apartment, you could also consider purchasing renter's insurance to cover the beneficiary's personal items in the event of fire, theft, or other loss.

Obtain Professional Help with Investments

In most states, a new trustee is supposed to review the trust assets and decide which ones to keep and which ones to sell. The initial review must be done within a reasonable time after the trustee takes over managing the trust. (This is required by the Uniform Prudent Investor Act, which has been adopted in most states.) We suggest that you hire a qualified financial adviser to assist you with this task.

In addition to reviewing the trust assets, a financial adviser can perform other important functions such as:

- Help you set-up a budget for the trust. This is important, because you don't want to risk running out of money while the beneficiary is still living.

- Suggest a strategy for investing the trust funds so they will earn a reasonable rate of return. A trustee has a specific duty to make the trust funds productive. You can't just let them sit in a checking account where they don't earn any interest.

- Take over investing the assets, if there are sufficient funds in the trust.

Information on working with a financial adviser is located in Chapter 12, "Investments."

Chapter 3
Supplemental Security Income (SSI)

Many people with disabilities rely on the Supplemental Security Income (SSI) program for their support. Recipients can receive a monthly check for several hundred dollars. In many states, SSI recipients can also receive Medicaid, which provides comprehensive medical benefits.

The SSI financial rules are strict. If a person has too much income or too many resources, he or she cannot obtain benefits, no matter how great the degree of disability. The financial rules are also complicated. In some cases, if you (the trustee) spend any money from the trust, the beneficiary's SSI payment may be reduced or completely eliminated. This can occur even if you do not give any money directly to the beneficiary. Thus, if the beneficiary receives SSI, it is critical for you to understand this program. This chapter explains the essential elements of SSI.

Overview of SSI

SSI is a federal program that pays monthly cash benefits to people who are elderly, blind, or have disabilities. SSI is funded from the general revenues of the United States Treasury and is run by the Social Security Administration, a federal agency. SSI benefits are sometimes referred to as Title XVI benefits.

In many states, SSI recipients automatically receive Medicaid. Note that Medicaid is NOT the same thing as Medicare. (Medicare is discussed in detail in Chapter 4, "SSDI, Medicare, and Medicaid.") Medicaid is a federally and state funded medical insurance program that is run by the states. The rules vary from state to state. Most states give their Medicaid programs a special name, such as MassHealth in Massachusetts and MediCal in California.

Medicaid pays for most medical treatments, including hospital care, doctor visits, and prescription drugs. For many adults with disabilities, Medicaid is the only insurance program that pays for residential services, day habilitation programs, and transportation between home and work or a day program. In fact, for some recipients, the Medicaid benefits that the SSI program automatically confers in most states are more important than the monthly cash payment. Medicaid is discussed in more detail in Chapter 4, "SSDI, Medicare, and Medicaid."

Benefit Amounts

The SSI benefit amount is set by the federal government on January 1 of each year. In 2010, an individual who qualifies can receive a maximum of $674 per month, and a married couple can receive a maximum of $1,011.[8] The monthly payment may be reduced if the person has any earnings or receives any cash, food, or housing-related items. This is explained in the "Income Limits" section of this chapter.

Currently nine states and the District of Columbia supplement the federal SSI benefit. Those states are California, Hawaii, Massachusetts, Nevada, New Jersey, New York, Pennsylvania, Rhode Island, and Vermont. In those states, recipients receive one monthly check that contains both the federal benefit and the state supplement.

Qualifying for SSI

To qualify for SSI, a person must:

- Have limited income and few resources, and
- Be elderly, blind, or medically disabled according to Social Security's rules (see below), and
- Initially, be not working, or working but earning less than $1,000 per month (in 2010), and
- Be a U.S. citizen or have the necessary immigrant status

To be considered medically disabled, a person must have a severe physical or mental impairment or combination of impairments:

[8] Social Security calls the payment amount the Federal Benefit Rate, or FBR.

- That have lasted, or can be expected to last, for a continuous period of at least 12 months, or
- Will result in death

[20 C.F.R. § 416.905]

The impairment must affect the person's ability to work and support himself or herself. The government calls the ability to support oneself through work "substantial gainful activity." The Social Security Administration has established certain earnings levels as reasonable signs that a person can support oneself through work. For the year 2010, that level is $1,000 per month for a non-blind person, and $1,640 per month for a blind person. These levels are indexed to an annual cost of living allowance and adjusted in January of each year. If a person can potentially earn $1,000 per month or more (or $1,640 or more if blind), Social Security presumes that he or she is able to be self-supporting.

Resource Limits

To receive SSI, a person may not own more than $2,000 in countable resources. A couple may only own $3,000. Social Security distinguishes between *countable* and *non-countable* resources.

A *countable* resource is generally defined as cash or other liquid asset or real property that the person owns and could convert to cash. [20 C.F.R. § 416.1201]

Examples of *countable* resources are:

- Cash (not including the current month's income) and bank accounts
- Income-producing property, including real estate (but not one's residence)
- Stocks, bonds, and other investments
- Life insurance with a cash value in excess of $1,500

Examples of *non-countable* resources are:

- Personal residence (including a condominium)
- Automobile, regardless of its value
- Personal property (furniture, home furnishings, computer, etc.), regardless of its aggregate value
- Assets in a Plan for Achieving Self-Support (PASS), described in Chapter 5, "SSI and Work"
- Burial insurance
- Life insurance with a cash value of less than $1,500
- Assets held in a properly drafted special needs trust

Income limits

A person's SSI payment may be reduced if he or she receives any income. Social Security considers three kinds of income: *unearned, earned,* and *in-kind.*

Unearned Income

Unearned income is income that is not received from work. Unearned income includes periodic payments such as Social Security benefits, annuities, alimony, child support, dividends, interest from bank accounts, royalties, rents, and one-time items such as prizes, awards, and gifts. Any distributions of cash from a special needs trust to the recipient are considered unearned income. [20 C.F.R. §§ 416.1120; 416.1121]

An SSI recipient may only receive up to $20 per month of unearned income without penalty. Any unearned income in excess of $20 per month will be deducted from the SSI benefit on a dollar-for-dollar basis.

> John lives independently and receives SSI of $674 per month. However, in one month, the trustee gives him $500 from the trust funds. That month, John's SSI benefit will be reduced by $480. This is calculated as follows:

$500.00	unearned income
-$20.00	SSI General Exclusion ($20)
$480.00	total countable unearned income

That month, John receives a reduced SSI benefit of $194, calculated as follows:

$674.00	SSI benefit
-$480.00	less total countable unearned income
$194.00	reduced SSI benefit

Earned Income

Earned income is earnings from wages or self-employment. Payment for work performed in a sheltered workshop is included within the definition of earned income. [20 C.F.R. § 416.1110]

In most cases, if an SSI recipient earns more than $65 per month (or $85 per month if there is no unearned income), his or her SSI benefit will be reduced. However, there are several exceptions to this rule, which are discussed in Chapter 5, "SSI and Work." One such exception is for students, who are permitted to earn up to $1,640 per month (up to a maximum of $6,600 per year in 2010) and still receive SSI. The earnings can be through a school job, or a regular job during the summer or on weekends. For purposes of SSI, a student is an individual who takes classes each week for at least eight hours in college; 12 hours in high school; or 15 hours in a vocational setting. [SI00820.510]

If none of the exceptions apply and there is any earned income, Social Security will disregard the first $65 and one-half of the remaining income. If the person has no unearned income, an additional $20 will be disregarded.

Dan lives independently and earns $200 per month from a part-time job. If Dan did not work, he would receive SSI of $674 per month. However, his benefit is reduced due to his earnings. The reduction is calculated as follows:

$200.00	earned income
-$20.00	SSI General Exclusion ($20)
$180.00	remaining earned income
-$65.00	SSI earned income disregard ($65)
$115.00	remaining earned income
-$57.50	less one-half of remaining earned income
$57.50	total countable earned income

That month, Dan receives a reduced SSI benefit of $616.60, calculated as follows:

$674.00	SSI benefit
-$57.50	less total countable earned income
$616.50	reduced SSI benefit

In-kind Income

In-kind income is any food or shelter item that an SSI recipient receives for free or at a reduced cost from a third party, including his or her special needs trust. The Social Security rules define in-kind income as "not cash, but food or shelter, or something the recipient can use to get one of those items." [20 C.F.R. §§416.1102; 417.1130] In-kind income is sometimes called "in-kind support and maintenance" or ISM.

Social Security considers the following items to be "countable" shelter expenses that will reduce the SSI benefit:

- mortgage (principal and interest)
- rent
- real estate taxes
- heating fuel
- gas
- electricity
- water

- sewer
- garbage removal
- homeowner's insurance (if required by a lender)
- condominium charges that include any of the above items

[20 C.F.R. § 1130(b); POMS SI 00835.465D]

If a recipient receives any of these shelter items for free or at a reduced cost from a third party, the SSI benefit may be reduced. This is true even if the third party is the recipient's special needs trust. Social Security has a complicated formula to figure the amount of the reduction: It is the lesser of the item's cost or one-third of the monthly SSI benefit plus twenty dollars.[9]

> Sarah lives in a condominium that her mother owns. The market rent is $900 per month, but Sarah only pays $300. Although Sarah receives $600 of "free" rent, Social Security only counts $244 ($674 x 1/3 + $20 = $244). Thus, Sarah has countable in-kind income of $244. For every month that Sarah receives reduced rent, her monthly benefit will be reduced by $244.

Fortunately, regardless of the amount of in-kind income, the SSI benefit is never reduced by more than one-third of the monthly benefit amount plus $20 ($244 in 2010). Thus, in the above example, even if the fair market rental of Sarah's condominium were $1,000 (so that Sarah receives $700 of "free" rent), the maximum deduction would not exceed $244. Also, note that the reduction only applies to the federal SSI benefit. In states that supplement the federal benefit, the state supplement is not reduced.

If an SSI recipient lives in someone else's home and receives free food and shelter, Social Security will automatically reduce the monthly benefit by one-third, regardless of the actual value of the food and

[9] This is called the Presumed Maximum Value Rule. See 20 C.F.R. § 1140; POMS SI 00835.300.

shelter.[10] A common example involves an adult (age 18 or older) who lives with his or her parents or other family members and does not contribute to the household costs. Social Security presumes that the food and shelter are worth at least one-third of the monthly benefit amount ($224 in 2010) and automatically reduces the monthly benefit by that amount.

> David lives with his parents and receives SSI of $450 per month (in 2010). If David lived alone, he would receive $674 per month. However, his benefit has been reduced due to the free food and shelter he receives from his parents. ($674 - $224 = $450)

Strategies to Avoid Reducing SSI

With all these complicated rules, it can be quite challenging to spend any money from the trust without affecting the beneficiary's SSI stipend. However, the following strategies should work.

Do not Give the Beneficiary any Cash

You should avoid giving any cash to a beneficiary who receives SSI. As we explained earlier in this chapter, if you give the beneficiary more than $20 in cash in any month, his or her SSI benefit will be reduced dollar for dollar for that month.

> John receives SSI and has no other income. The trustee gives him $100. That month, John's SSI benefit will be reduced by $80. (Social Security disregards the first $20 of unearned income.)

In the above example, even if the trustee gave John $2,500, he would only lose SSI for that month. The next month, he would receive the full

[10] This is called the One-Third Reduction Rule. See 20 C.F.R. §416.1131; POMS SI 00835.200.

SSI benefit. This is because Social Security counts income on a monthly basis. The next month's benefit is not affected. This assumes, of course, that John spent the $2,500 and did not keep it. If he kept the $2,500, he would have more than $2,000 in countable resources and would lose SSI until the resources were reduced to $2,000 or less.

Avoid Giving the Beneficiary any Food or Shelter Items

An SSI recipient is expected to pay for all food and shelter costs from the SSI stipend. As we explained earlier in this chapter, if you give an SSI recipient any food or shelter items, his or her SSI benefit will be reduced. The amount of the reduction is the item's actual value or one-third of the monthly SSI benefit plus $20 ($244 in 2010), whichever is less.

> Christine lives in her own apartment. The trustee buys groceries for Christine that cost $100. Christine's SSI benefit will be reduced by $80. (The first $20 of unearned income is disregarded.)
>
> Erica lives in her own apartment. One month, the trustee pays her landlord $500. Erica's SSI benefit for that month will be reduced by $244.

Fortunately, the monthly SSI benefit may never be reduced by more than $244 (in 2010), no matter how much in-kind income the recipient receives. In the above example, if the trustee paid Erica's landlord $750, Erica's SSI benefit would still only be reduced by $244.

Pay the Beneficiary's Bills Instead of Giving Him or Her Money to Pay the Bills

If the beneficiary incurs any expenses that are not in-kind expenses for food or shelter, you should pay the creditor directly. That way, the beneficiary is "out of the loop," and SSI will not be affected.

> Melanie, an SSI recipient, needs dental care costing $350. The trustee pays the dentist directly. Melanie's SSI benefit is not affected. But if the trustee gave Melanie $350 to pay the dentist, Melanie's SSI benefit would be reduced by $330 ($350 if Melanie had other unearned income).

Note, again, that the strategy of paying a creditor directly will not work for food or shelter items. If you pay more than $20 in any month for either of those items, the beneficiary's SSI benefit will be reduced.

> Chris has an overdue electric bill. The trustee writes a check for $500 payable to the utility company. That month, Chris's SSI benefit will be reduced by $244. The maximum monthly reduction is $244 (in 2010).

Children's Benefits

Children who are blind or have other disabilities can qualify for SSI. However, in addition to the income and resource counting rules described earlier in this chapter, other special financial eligibility rules apply. Until the child reaches age 18, a portion of the income and resources of parents who live with the child may be attributed ("deemed") to the child for eligibility purposes. [20 C.F.R. §416.1160] For deeming purposes, there are certain resource limits for both the child and the parent or parents. For example, the resource limit for a two-parent household is $5,000 ($4,000 for a one-parent household). Because of these strict deeming rules, many children with disabilities cannot receive SSI until their eighteenth birthdays, when they can qualify under the adult rules.

There are also different disability rules for children. Since a work test does not make sense for children, Social Security looks for a mental or physical impairment, or combination of impairments, that substantially affects the child's ability to reach age appropriate developmental milestones, or to engage in age appropriate activities of daily living. Essentially, Social Security compares the functioning of SSI applicant children to that of same age children without disabilities. [20 C.F.R §

416.924] Social Security reviews a child's file annually to determine if he or she still qualifies for benefits.

Keeping Track of Recipients' Finances

Trustees sometimes wonder how the Social Security Administration keeps track of its recipients' finances. The agency has several ways to obtain financial information.

- Sharing information with other government agencies. Social Security routinely shares information with other government agencies. Social Security can find out from the Internal Revenue Service whether any income has been reported under a recipient's Social Security Number. This will alert the agency that a recipient has worked or owns assets that are generating interest or dividends. Social Security also shares information with the Medicare and Medicaid programs. Social Security is interested in such information because, in some cases, a recipient who has spent a full calendar month in a medical facility (hospital, rehabilitation facility, etc.) is not entitled to receive an SSI benefit that month. [20 C.F.R. 416.211, SI 00520.001]

- Voluntary reporting. The agency relies on recipients to provide information. Recipients must report any changes to income or assets within ten days.

- Periodic reviews. The agency conducts periodic reviews to make sure that recipients still meet the disability and financial requirements. Recipients may be asked to come to the local office and bring financial records like pay stubs, W-2 forms, and bank statements. If the recipient is the beneficiary of a trust, he or she will probably be asked to bring copies of the trust bank statements and records that show how the trust funds were spent.

It is the beneficiary or his or her *representative payee* — not the trustee — who deals directly with Social Security.[11] Unless you happen to be the representative payee, you are not required to report to the agency. Nevertheless, if the beneficiary's case is being reviewed and he or she asks you for information about the trust, it is important to provide the information promptly. If you do not, the beneficiary could lose his or her SSI benefit.

[11] The representative payee is the person Social Security designates to receive the government benefit checks on the recipient's behalf. The agency can appoint a "rep payee" if a recipient needs assistance to manage the government benefits.

CHAPTER 4
SSDI, Medicare and Medicaid

In addition to SSI, there are other public benefit programs that support people with disabilities. This chapter explains Social Security Disability, Medicare, and Medicaid.

Social Security Disability Insurance (SSDI)

The definition of disability for the SSDI program is the same as for the SSI program. To be considered medically disabled, a person must have a severe physical or mental impairment or combination of impairments:

- That have lasted, or can be expected to last, for a continuous period of at least 12 months, or
- Will result in death

[42 U.S.C. § 416(i)(1)]

It is much easier to manage a special needs trust if the beneficiary receives SSDI than if he or she receives SSI. For one thing, with SSDI, there is no $2,000 resource limit. In fact, there is no resource test at all. An SSDI recipient can own significant assets and still qualify for benefits. Also, there is no limit on the amount of assistance an SSDI recipient can receive from his or her trust. This is because Social Security only considers earnings from work. You (the trustee) can give the beneficiary unlimited amounts of cash or spend the trust funds on food or shelter without reducing the SSDI benefit.

Some SSDI recipients also receive SSI. (This is explained later in this chapter.) If the beneficiary for whom you are managing the trust receives income from both of those programs, you must be careful not to inadvertently reduce the SSI benefit. This means you should try not to give the beneficiary any cash or pay for any food or housing items from the trust funds, because doing so will reduce SSI.

Who can qualify for benefits?

- A worker who becomes medically disabled can collect benefits based on his or her own work record. To qualify, a person must not be working (or, if working, earning less than $1,000 per month in 2010). A person must also have worked a sufficient number of quarters of "covered" employment before becoming disabled. In general, that means one must have accrued 20 quarters of employment that were earned in the last 10 years ending with the year the disability began.

- A minor (under age 18) dependent of a disabled, retired, or deceased worker can collect benefits through age 18, or through age 21 if enrolled in school.

- The disabled son or daughter of a disabled, retired, or deceased worker can receive benefits for life.[12] To qualify, the son's or daughter's disability must have started before age 22 and remained continuous through the time that he or she is claiming benefits.

  Jonathan, who is age 25 and has developmental disabilities, can collect SSDI benefits based on his father's work record when his father begins to draw benefits.

  Melissa, who became disabled in a car accident when she was 25, cannot receive SSDI *based on her parent's work record* because she was not continuously disabled since before age 22.

Benefit Amounts

The amount of SSDI benefits a dependent with a disability can receive is based on his or her parent's benefit. That benefit is set according to

[12] Social Security calls a disabled son or daughter who is age 18 or older a "disabled adult child" (DAC).

the parent's earnings record. In order for the dependent to receive benefits, the parent must be drawing benefits. Another important point is that the dependent's award is *in addition to* the parent's benefit. It does not reduce the parent's benefit. If not reduced by the Family Maximum Benefit (see below), a dependent with a disability receives 50 percent of the parent's benefit while the parent is living and 75 percent of the benefit after the parent has died.

The amount a dependent may receive is subject to a "Family Maximum Benefit" that Social Security establishes for each insured worker. If a disabled, retired, or deceased worker has dependent family members, the total benefits payable to both the worker and the family members may not exceed a Family Maximum Benefit. The family members may include a spouse, unmarried children under age 18 (up to age 19 if a full-time student), and adult children with disabilities. The worker is always paid first. The worker's benefit is not reduced by any family members' benefits. Upon request, Social Security can tell a person the approximate amounts the family would receive in the event of disability, retirement, or death.

Recipients of both SSDI and SSI ("Dual Recipients")

Some people receive both SSDI benefits and SSI benefits each month. This might occur if the amount of SSDI the person receives is lower than the SSI benefit the person is entitled to receive. In that case, the person's combined SSDI and SSI benefit must equal the maximum SSI entitlement.

> Robert, who lives independently, is receiving SSI benefits of $674 per month. Then his father retires and Robert becomes entitled to receive $500 of SSDI benefits based on his father's work record. Robert's SSI benefit will be reduced by $480 due to the income from SSDI. (Social Security disregards $20 of SSDI income and counts $480. So, $500 - $20 = $480.) Robert will receive $194 in SSI benefits. ($674 - $480 = $194) Robert will receive $694 in combined SSDI and SSD benefits (SSDI of $500 + SSI of $194 = $694).

Comparison of SSI and SSDI		
	SSI	*SSDI*
Asset limit	Yes	No
Limit on earned income	Yes	Yes, if $1,000/ mo. or more (in 2010)
Limit on unearned income	Yes	No
Benefit can fluctuate each month	Yes, if there is earned or unearned income	No
Entitlement based on financial need	Yes	No
Automatic Medicare entitlement	No	Yes, after 24 months
Automatic Medicaid entitlement	Yes, in most states	No

No Asset Limit

Unlike the SSI program, there is no asset limit for SSDI. A person can have significant assets and still receive SSDI.

SSDI and Unearned Income

The SSDI program does not consider any unearned income the individual may receive. A person can have income from an annuity, rental property, or investment account without affecting SSDI. A person can also receive cash from his or her trust without affecting SSDI.

SSDI and In-kind Income

The SSDI program does not consider in-kind income. Any payments you (the trustee) make to third parties who assist the beneficiary will not reduce the SSDI benefit.

SSDI and Medicare

SSDI recipients can obtain Medicare after they have qualified for SSDI for 24 months. (The Medicare program is discussed later in this chapter.)

SSDI and Medicaid

SSDI recipients do NOT automatically qualify for Medicaid benefits. SSDI recipients must qualify separately for Medicaid under their state's rules.

SSDI and Work

Earnings from employment and self-employment are treated differently under the SSDI program than under the SSI program. With SSI, a person's benefit can fluctuate from month to month depending on the amount of earnings. However, SSDI remains constant if the person earns less than $1,000 per month (in 2010).[13] If a person earns more than that amount, his or her SSDI benefit may end altogether. Another important point is that SSDI is never partially reduced. A recipient collects either the entire check or none at all.

---

[13] If a non-blind person can earn more than $1,000 per month, Social Security will presume that the person is able to support himself or herself through employment ("substantial gainful activity"). SGA is discussed in Chapter 3, "SSI."

> Ben receives SSDI of $895 per month based on his retired father's earnings. Ben also has earnings of $750 per month from a part-time job. Ben can keep all his earnings, because $750 is below the $1,000 per month limit on earned income.
>
> If Ben earned $1,000 per month, he might lose his SSDI benefits altogether. This is because he has exceeded the earnings limit of $1,000 per month (in 2010) and is presumed to be capable of self-support.

Fortunately, Social Security has enacted several "work incentive" programs that allow a person to earn more than $1,000 per month and still receive SSDI. These include Impairment-Related Work Expenses (discussed in Chapter 5, "SSI and Work,"), the Trial Work Period, and the Extended Period of Eligibility. Some important work incentives are just for SSDI recipients and others specifically assist SSI recipients. The government's policy is to encourage people who can work to do so. A good source of information on these programs is Social Security's "Red Book on Employment," which is listed in the Chapter 16, "Resources." The Red Book is comprehensive, easy to read, and provides many helpful examples.

Medicare

Medicare is a federally funded medical insurance program. People who have qualified for SSDI for 24 months can receive Medicare for themselves and their dependents. Social Security retirees who are age 65 and older can receive Medicare as part of their retirement benefit. Medicare has several parts. This section explains parts A, B, C, and D. There is additional information on the Medicare websites (http://www.medicare.gov and http://www.cms.hhs.gov).

Medicare Part A

Medicare Part A covers charges for semi-private hospital room and board up to 60 days, subject to an annual deductible ($1,100 in 2010). For stays that last between 61 and 90 days, recipients pay co-insurance of $275 per day; and for stays between 91 and 150 days, recipients pay $550 per day. Medicare does not pay for stays of more than 150 days.

Medicare Part A also covers 20 days of skilled nursing care in a facility such as a rehabilitation hospital or nursing home that has been approved by Medicare. After 20 days, recipients must pay co-insurance ($137.50 per day in 2010). After 100 days, Medicare will not pay for any skilled care in a nursing home.

For most participants, part A is free. However, because of the high co-insurance payments, recipients should consider purchasing supplemental (Medigap) insurance. This kind of insurance is offered by private insurers in all 50 states.

Medicare Part B

Medicare Part B pays for physician services, hospital outpatient care, lab services, medical equipment, psychiatric care, physical and occupational therapy, and some preventive services.

Most participants pay a monthly premium of $96.40 in 2010. (The premiums are higher for individuals who earn over $85,000 and couples who earn over $170,000.) Participants also pay an annual $155 deductible for all Part B services. Medicare recipients with very low income and few assets can qualify for state assistance in paying the Medicare B premiums and deductibles (discussed later in this chapter).

Medicare determines an allowable charge (the "approved amount") for Part B services and pays 80 percent of that amount. The remaining 20 percent is paid by the participant. These amounts change if the participant does not elect Medicare Part C (discussed below). Participants can purchase supplemental coverage (Medigap insurance) through a private insurance company to cover any amounts Medicare does not pay for.

Medicare Part C

Medicare Part C, also called Medicare Advantage, is Medicare's version of managed care. Medicare pays doctors and other medical providers who join a Medicare Advantage Plan a fixed amount of money each year to manage the participant's care. Participants enroll with a private health insurance plan (Blue Cross/Blue Shield, Humana, etc.). Participants may be restricted to using doctors in the plan's network. In exchange for this limitation, participants may get additional benefits such as extra days in the hospital and coverage for some prescription drugs. Each Medicare Advantage Plan sets its own terms, conditions, and costs.

Medicare Part D

Medicare Part D is the prescription drug benefit. Prescription drug coverage is available to anyone who is enrolled in Medicare. Medicare Part D is run through private drug plans known as Prescription Drug Plans (PDPs). Each PDP has different coverage, terms, premiums, and deductible amounts. Also, Medicare drug plans have a "coverage gap," which is sometimes referred to as the "donut hole." A coverage gap means that after the member has spent a certain amount of money for drugs (no more than $3,850), he or she must pay for all drug costs while in the "gap." The maximum the person must pay while in the coverage gap is $3,052. Once the member has reached the plan's out-of-pocket limit, the person only has to pay a coinsurance amount (about 5% of the drug cost) or a co-payment for the rest of the calendar year. The co-payments are set by each PDP.

Individuals who qualify for both Medicaid and Medicare must obtain their prescription drug coverage under Medicare Part D. Medicaid will not pay for any prescription drugs for these individuals. However, to mitigate the financial hardship, Medicare will provide "extra help" to pay prescription drug costs, including the monthly premiums, annual deductible, and co-payments. There are full and partial subsidies. To qualify for a full subsidy in 2010, a single person's income cannot exceed $12,910 ($14,620 for a married couple), and countable resources cannot exceed $14,620 ($19,669 for a couple). The income and resource limits change annually. Individuals can apply for extra help at any Social Security office on online at http://www.benefitscheckup.org. Some individuals can also qualify for assistance in paying for Medicare premiums, deductibles, and co-payments through their state's Medicaid program (see below).

Medicaid

Medicaid, which is also known as Medical Assistance, provides comprehensive medical services to individuals who qualify. Medicaid can be an important source of payment for basic medical care and prescription medications. In many states, adults with disabilities also receive residential services, day habilitation support, and transportation through the Medicaid program.

If the beneficiary receives Medicaid — or could potentially benefit from that program — it is critical for you to understand the Medicaid program rules. Although Medicaid is partially funded by the federal government, the states are given a great deal of leeway to set their own rules. The rules can vary from state to state.

State rules may be different depending on whether the recipient lives in an institution (such as a rehabilitation facility, state hospital or nursing home) or in the community (such as with family, in his or her own apartment, or in a group home). Some states even have different rules for employed and unemployed individuals. It is important to understand the rules in the state where the beneficiary lives. You can find information on the state's website, and your attorney will have this information as well. You will need to know:

- Will the existence of the special needs trust cause a problem for the beneficiary?

- Are there any limits on assets? Some states place limits on the amount of assets a Medicaid recipient can own, such as a bank account, automobile, or household items. If that is the case in your state, you must be careful about purchasing assets for the beneficiary that might cause him or her to exceed the program's asset limit.

- Are there any limits on income? Some states place limits on the amount of income a Medicaid recipient can receive. If the person's income is too high, he or she might not qualify for benefits. In addition, there might be a monthly premium for coverage based on the person's income. You need to know whether any money you spend from the trust might cause the beneficiary to lose Medicaid or pay higher premiums. Also, you need to understand how the state rules define "income." Does it only mean money you pay directly to the beneficiary? Or does it include money you pay to third parties for the beneficiary's bills (such as rent, utilities, car payments, etc.)? The state's definition of income will be included within its program rules, which most states post on their websites. Your attorney can also explain the income rules for your state.

Basic Services

The services that Medicaid will cover vary from state to state. However, the states must provide the following services:

- Inpatient hospital care
- Outpatient hospital care
- Physician services
- Laboratory and x-ray services
- Certified pediatric and family nurse practitioners
- Family planning services and supplies
- Nurse midwife services
- Skilled nursing facility services (such as nursing homes) for persons over age 21
- Dental services (medical and surgical only)
- Home health care services for persons over age 21 who are entitled to nursing facility services under the state's Medicaid plan

- Early and periodic screening, diagnosis and treatment (EPSDT) for individuals under age 21
- Pregnancy-related services and 60 days of postpartum care

Comparison of Medicare and Medicaid

	Medicare	*Medicaid*
Automatic entitlement with SSI	No	Yes, in most states
Automatic entitlement with SSDI	Yes, after qualifying for SSDI for 24 mo.	No
Asset limit	No	In most states
Limit on earned income	No	In most states
Pays for doctors, hospitals, hospitals, lab tests, etc.	Yes	Yes
Pays for adult day habilitation programs	No	In some states
Pays for residential services for adults with disibilities	No	In some states
Pays for institutional care	Skilled care only (not custodial)	Yes
Pays for prescription drugs	Yes, subject to deductibles and co-payments	In some states

Some states may provide additional items and services such as routine dental care, physical therapy, optometrist services, eyeglasses, occupational therapy, and transportation. To find out what services your state will cover, check with the state's Medicaid office.

Medicaid and SSI

In many states, and in the District of Columbia, SSI recipients automatically qualify for Medicaid. The states that confer automatic eligibility are: Alabama, Arizona, Arkansas, California, Colorado, Delaware, Florida, Georgia, Iowa, Kentucky, Louisiana, Maine, Maryland, Massachusetts, Michigan, Mississippi, Montana, New Jersey, New Mexico, New York, North Carolina, Pennsylvania, Rhode Island, South Carolina, South Dakota, Tennessee, Texas, Vermont, Washington, West Virginia, Wisconsin, and Wyoming.

In seven states, SSI recipients must apply separately for Medicaid; however, the same eligibility rules apply for both programs. The states are: Alaska, Idaho, Kansas, Nebraska, Nevada, Oregon, and Utah.

Eleven states use their own eligibility rules for Medicaid, which are different from the Social Security Administration's rules for SSI. SSI recipients in these states must file a separate application in order to receive Medicaid. These states are: Connecticut, Hawaii, Illinois, Indiana, Minnesota, Missouri, New Hampshire, North Dakota, Ohio, Oklahoma, and Virginia. You can obtain information on how to apply for Medicaid benefits by calling the state's Medicaid office or going to its website.

Medicaid Payment of Medicare Premiums and Costs

If the beneficiary has little income and few personal assets ($4,000 for an individual and $6,000 for a couple), find out if the state Medicaid program will pay for the person's Medicare Parts A and B premiums, deductibles, and coinsurance payments. There are four other programs that will help with these kinds of costs, depending on the person's (or couple's) income:

- Qualified Medicare Beneficiary (QMB). Pays Part A and Part B premiums, deductibles, co-insurance, and co-payments. The monthly income limit is $923 for an individual and $1,235 for a couple.

- Specified Low-Income Medicare Beneficiary (SLMB). Pays Part B premiums for individuals with monthly incomes of not more than $1,103 ($1,447 for a couple).

- Qualifying Individual (QI). Pays Part B premiums for individuals with monthly incomes of not more than $1,239 ($1,660 for a couple).

- Qualified Disabled and Working Individuals (QDWI). Pays Part A premiums for individuals with monthly incomes of not more than $3,695 ($4,942 for a couple).

The eligibility figures are based roughly on the federal poverty level (FPL), which can be located on the website for the U.S. Department of Health and Human Services (http://www.aspe.hhs.gov/poverty). The FPL is adjusted annually. The 2010 figures are available on the federal Medicaid website (http://www.cms.gov).

CHAPTER 5
SSI and Work

When an SSI recipient gets a job, his earnings can work against him for SSI purposes. As earnings increase, SSI benefits go down and may stop altogether if earnings are too high.

This reduction in benefits is logical because SSI is a program for people with disabilities who are unable to be "gainfully employed." In judging whether a person can perform gainful employment, Social Security uses an earnings test. As a general rule, if a person can earn more than $1,000 per month in 2010 ($1,640 if blind), then he or she is presumed to be capable of gainful employment and cannot get SSI. However, Social Security has enacted several "work incentive" programs to encourage SSI recipients to work. These programs allow recipients to earn more than $1,000 per month and still receive SSI. This chapter discusses some of those programs. (There are additional work-related publications and websites in Chapter 16, "Resources.")

Excluded Student Earnings

If an SSI recipient is under age 22 and regularly attends school, Social Security will exclude up to $1,640 of earnings per month (up to a maximum of $6,600 per calendar year) in 2010. For SSI purposes, "regularly attending school" means that a person takes one or more courses of study and attends classes:

- In a college or university for at least eight hours a week, or
- In grades 7-12 for at least 12 hours a week, or
- In a training course to prepare for employment for at least twelve hours a week (15 hours a week if the course involves "shop" practice), or
- For less time than indicated above for reasons beyond the student's control, such as illness.

Sean, who is age 19 and a special education student, works on Saturdays at an auto body shop. He earns $70 per week, and in 2010, he earned $3,500 from this job. Sean's SSI benefit is not affected, because $3,500 is below the $6,600 maximum allowable earnings.

Earned Income Exclusion

Social Security does not count the first $65 per month of a recipient's earnings. Also, one-half of any earnings over $65 per month are not counted.

Sharon, age 25, earns $430 per month from a part-time job. If Sharon did not work, she would receive SSI of $674 per month. However, her monthly benefit has been reduced by $172.50 due to her earnings. The reduction is calculated as follows:

$430.00	earned income
-$20.00	SSI General Exclusion ($20)
$410.00	remaining earned income
-$65.00	SSI earned income disregard ($65)
$345.00	remaining earned income
-$172.50	less one-half of remaining earned income
$172.50	total countable earned income
$674.00	SSI benefit
-$172.50	less total countable earned income
$501.50	reduced SSI benefit

Sharon will have $931.50 per month available for her self-support (earnings of $430 plus SSI of $501.50).

Impairment-Related Work Expenses

If a person needs special items or services in order to work, the expenses can be deducted from the person's earnings when SSI is calculated. In most cases, this is true even if the items and services are also needed for normal daily activities. Some examples of Impairment-Related Work Expenses (IRWE) include:

- accessibility modifications to a residence
- attendant care services
- equipment, such as a wheelchair
- guide dog
- medical devices and supplies

To qualify as an Impairment-Related Work Expense, the item or service must be directly related to the person's work. Even if the person uses the item or service for both work and normal daily activities, the entire item or service can qualify. An exception is personal care attendant services. For example, a person who works might need an attendant every day to help him get up, get dressed, and bathe. The attendant's services on work days would be deductible, but not on non-work days.

The following example illustrates how an Impairment-Related Work Expense can offset income, allowing a person to increase his total income from earnings and SSI.

> Frank earns $500 per month in supported employment and has no unearned income. His IRWE are $250 per month.

$500.00	earned income
-$20.00	SSI General Exclusion ($20)
$480.00	remaining earned income
-$65.00	SSI earned income disregard ($65)
$415.00	remaining earned income

-$250.00	less IRWE
$165.00	remaining earned income
-$82.50	less one-half of remaining earned income
$82.50	remaining earned income
$674.00	SSI benefit
-$82.50	less total countable earned income
$591.50	reduced SSI benefit

Frank has $841.50 per month available for his self-support. This consists of net earnings of $250 (gross earnings of $500 minus $250 IRWE) plus SSI of $591.50.

The Trustee Should not Pay for any Work-related Items

In order for a work-related item to be deductible, the SSI recipient must pay for it from his or her own funds. For example, let's say a worker needs special transportation. If a third party, such as the worker's family or his or her special needs trust, pays for the transportation expense, it would not be allowed as an IRWE. Thus, in order to maximize the recipient's SSI benefit, you (the trustee) should not use the trust funds to pay for any items or services that could qualify as impairment-related work expenses. Instead, the recipient should pay for these expenses from his or her own earnings, if that is possible.

Plan for Achieving Self-Support (PASS)

A Plan to Achieve Self-Support (PASS) is a way that a person with a disability can set aside income or resources, or both, while working toward an occupational goal. While a PASS is in place, a person can earn more income and retain more resources than would ordinarily be the case with SSI. Social Security must approve a PASS before it can be put into place. Also, there are specific guidelines that must be followed. A PASS must:

- Be designed specifically for the person's own needs, goals, abilities, and other circumstances.

- Be in writing and signed by the person for whom it is written.

- Have a designated and feasible work goal that states the person's proposed job, that he or she has a reasonable chance of getting and keeping the job, and will earn additional income that is enough to achieve self-support.

- Have a timetable for achieving the goal (the initial period cannot exceed 18 months, but with extensions, the PASS can continue for 48 months total).

- Show what income and resources the person has and will receive that will be used to achieve the work goal, and how the income and resources will be used.

- Show how the money set aside for resources will be kept identifiable from other money the person owns.

The following example shows how a PASS can benefit a person who wants to become self-supporting.

> Maria, who receives SSI of $674 per month, is taking courses to become a lab assistant, with the goal of becoming self-supporting. During an internship, her salary will be $1,200 per month. She will have monthly expenses of $450 for child care and transportation. By using a PASS, Maria can collect the full SSI benefit during the training period. Without a PASS, Social Security would reduce Maria's benefit during her internship. The following shows the calculation:

$1,200.00	earned income
-$20.00	SSI General Exclusion ($20)

$1,180.00	remaining earned income
-$65.00	SSI earned income disregard ($65)
$1,115.00	remaining earned income
-$557.50	less one-half of remaining earned income
$557.50	total countable earned income
$674.00	SSI benefit
-$557.50	less total countable earned income
$116.50	reduced SSI benefit

Comparison of Benefits

	Not Working	Working without PASS	Working with PASS
Income	$0.00		
Salary	$0.00	$1,200.00	$1,200.00
SSI	$674	$116.00	$674.00
	$674	**$1,316.00**	**$1,874.00**
Expenses			
Child care and Transportation	$0.00	$450.00	$450.00
Net Income	**$674.00**	**$866.00**	**$1,424.00**

Chapter 6

Paying for Recreation, Transportation, Medical Expenses, and More

This chapter focuses on recreation, transportation, and medical care. Many beneficiaries seem to need help with these items at one time or another. We also explain an instance when you should not pay for any transportation or medical items — that is when an SSI or SSDI recipient needs them in order to work. We begin by suggesting some strategies you can use to purchase goods and services for the beneficiary.

Practical Strategies to Pay for Items the Beneficiary Needs

Trustees sometimes wonder what the best way is to pay for items the beneficiary needs. There is no single approach that you must always use. Instead, you may need to be creative and try different strategies. Any or all of the approaches listed below might work depending on the beneficiary's needs, level of ability, and living situation. Convenience is another factor — some of the strategies might be better suited for a family trustee who has close contact with the beneficiary rather than for a professional trustee who does not see the beneficiary very often.

You also need to consider the public assistance the beneficiary receives. You don't want to inadvertently disrupt the flow of public benefits. If the beneficiary receives SSDI, there should not be any problem, because the SSDI program does not consider assistance the person receives from a trust. But if the person receives SSI, you need to be careful. You should avoid giving the beneficiary cash or paying for any food or housing items. Recall from Chapter 3, "SSI," that if an SSI recipient receives cash of more than $20 per month, SSI will be reduced on a dollar for dollar basis. If the recipient receives any food or housing items, the monthly benefit can be reduced by up to one-third. (The maximum reduction in 2010 is $244 per month.)

Some beneficiaries receive *both* SSI *and* SSDI. In that case, even though you don't have to worry about reducing the SSDI benefit, you should still use one of the approaches listed below to avoid reducing the SSI payment.

With these caveats in mind, here are some strategies to consider:

- *Send payments directly to third parties.* You can send payments directly to third parties to pay for items like medical care, personal services, education courses, house cleaning, or a health club membership.

- *Give the beneficiary a monthly allowance.* This approach might work if the beneficiary can manage a small amount of money or has someone to help him or her manage the money. Giving the beneficiary an allowance will not work if the beneficiary receives SSI, because the SSI program rules do not allow a person to receive cash payments of more than $20 per month. You can send a check or transfer the funds directly from the trust bank account to the person's checking account. Besides being easy for the trustee, this approach can allow the beneficiary some privacy. Some beneficiaries do not want the trustee to know about the personal items they purchase. With a monthly allowance, the beneficiary pays the bills and the trustee doesn't necessarily know the details. If the beneficiary can't manage an allowance, perhaps you could pay someone a few hours a month to help him or her draw up a budget, shop, pay bills, and balance the checkbook. Sometimes the state office of disability services will provide someone or give a stipend to hire assistance.

- *Put money in the beneficiary's personal needs account.* If the beneficiary lives in a supervised arrangement like a group home or rehab facility, he or she might have a personal needs account. You can deposit funds in the account for the staff to give out. The staff might give the beneficiary a small amount of spending money (daily or weekly) to carry in a wallet for items like lunches, snacks, and drinks. The staff could also assist the beneficiary to shop for toiletries, clothes, a haircut, etc. You can replenish the personal needs account when the funds are depleted. A potential problem with putting money in the personal needs account is that if the beneficiary receives SSI, Social Security might treat the funds as distributions of cash. This could occur even though the source of funds is the beneficiary's own trust. However, one of the authors regularly deposits money in a beneficiary's personal needs account without any adverse consequences. She is careful to make the checks payable to the agency that oversees the beneficiary's care and to characterize them as distributions for recreation, enrichment, and necessities. To date, Social Security has not challenged these expenditures.

- *Have a third party take the beneficiary shopping.* You could have a friend or relative of the beneficiary take the person shopping and then reimburse him or her. The friend or relative could purchase and set-up a computer, television, DVD player, etc.

- *Obtain a trust credit card.* Some credit card companies will issue a credit card to a trust. You (the trustee) might have to furnish your personal guarantee. You could take the beneficiary shopping and pay for your purchases with the trust credit card. Alternatively, you could shop online for items like clothes, linens, or sports equipment and have the items sent to the beneficiary.

- *Arrange for the beneficiary to have a personal credit card — but not a debit card linked to the beneficiary's bank account.* The beneficiary could obtain his or her own credit card. The card should have a low maximum limit (say, $1,500) and not permit any cash withdrawals. The beneficiary and you should agree in advance on what the card will be used for. Some common items are public transportation, clothes, groceries (if SSI is not a factor), household cleaning products, prescription drugs, and toiletries. You can have the credit card company send the bill directly to you and then pay it from the trust funds.

If the beneficiary receives SSI, a risk with paying a monthly credit card bill is that Social Security could consider the recipient to have a regular source of income and reduce the benefit. Another risk is that the person might not use the card responsibly.

A caution: If the beneficiary receives SSI, make sure that the card he or she is using to make purchases is truly a credit card, and not a debit card that is linked to a bank account. If you use the trust funds to replenish the beneficiary's bank account, the SSI benefit will be reduced. To illustrate, let's say the beneficiary has his own bank account and obtains a debit card that he uses to buy $250 worth of clothes, toiletries, and household products. You put $250 into the bank account to replenish it. That month, the SSI benefit will be reduced by $230.[14] The funds you put in the beneficiary's personal bank account are considered a distribution of cash that will reduce SSI almost on a dollar for dollar basis. This is true even though the source of the funds is the beneficiary's trust.

Recreation Expenses

As trustees, we are sometimes asked to pay for recreation expenses. Paying for recreation items can be one of the more enjoyable aspects of managing a trust. The items listed below are some typical recreation expenses you may be asked to pay for:

- *Club Memberships.* Some people with disabilities belong to organizations like a local health club or YMCA. You could send a check from the trust account to pay the annual membership fees.

- *Movie and Concert Tickets.* Many people like to go out with friends to movies, sports events, and concerts. It is almost

[14] Social Security disregards the first $20 of monthly income.

always more convenient to have the beneficiary (or the person who is helping him or her) buy the tickets. The beneficiary can use his or her personal funds to pay for them. If more money is needed, you could ask the person accompanying the beneficiary to advance the money and then reimburse him or her.

- *Home entertainment.* A person doesn't necessarily need to go out to have fun. Some people like to stay home and watch television, rent movies, or listen to music. So if the beneficiary wants a big screen TV or home entertainment system, should you buy it? It's all right as far as Social Security is concerned. Currently there is no limit on the value of personal items an SSI recipient can own. (Before 2005, an SSI recipient could not own personal property that had an aggregate value of more than $2,000. However, that restriction has been removed.)

- *Paid Companions.* In order to enjoy a community experience, some people with disabilities may require one-to-one assistance from specially trained staff. These "paid companions" are usually compensated on an hourly basis. You can write a check from the trust fund to pay the person's fees.

- *Restaurant Meals.* Most people like to eat out. However, if the beneficiary receives SSI, paying for a restaurant meal can be challenging for a trustee. The SSI rules prohibit a recipient from receiving any food, or cash to buy food, from an "outside source" such as the special needs trust. Perhaps the beneficiary could use his or her own funds for meals, and you can use the trust funds for any non-food related items the person needs. Alternatively, if the person lives in a group setting, such as a group home, he or she could use the money in his or her personal needs account.

- *Vacations and Travel.* Some travel agencies offer package vacations adapted for people with disabilities. These include weekend trips, ski packages, and ocean cruises. Usually there is a single charge that covers airline, hotel, meals, and other amenities. Although a vacation package includes both food and shelter, which Social Security says are prohibited items, the current rules allow a recipient to receive food and shelter without penalty during a temporary absence from home, such as a vacation. A temporary absence is one of at least 24-hours duration. [20 C.F.C. § 416.1149; SI 00835.040]

Transportation

Some beneficiaries own a vehicle. If the beneficiary receives SSI, owning a vehicle will not interfere with the person's eligibility, regardless of the vehicle's value. Before 2005, there was a $4,500 limit on the vehicle's value unless it met certain requirements (i.e., it was adapted, or needed for medical care, or essential due to geography or terrain). Now, Social Security disregards the vehicle's value.

Paying for Transportation Costs

Perhaps the beneficiary needs help from the trust to pay for some or all of the vehicle's costs, such as gas, maintenance, repairs, and insurance. If the beneficiary receives SSI, paying these kinds of expenses will not affect the SSI benefit. But you can't give money directly to the beneficiary. Instead, you could provide the beneficiary with a gas credit card and pay the charges from the trust funds. The beneficiary should not use the credit card to pay for food or to obtain any cash advances, because this would reduce the SSI benefit.

Who Should Own the Beneficiary's Vehicle?

If you are planning to use the trust funds to buy a vehicle, you must decide who will own it. Below we list four options to consider: the beneficiary's parent, another relative, the beneficiary, or the special needs trust.

If you are buying an adapted vehicle such as a wheelchair accessible van, one factor to consider is vehicle taxes in your state. Adapted vehicles can be quite expensive, sometimes costing more than $50,000. The sales taxes in some states can be significant. Some states waive the sales tax if the owner has a disability, or if the owner is the parent of a child with a disability who will use the vehicle. Besides the sales tax, some states impose annual personal property taxes that are based on the vehicle's value. However, some states waive the annual taxes if the owner has a disability. You can get information on vehicle taxes from your state's registry of motor vehicles.

The following are the benefits and disadvantages of the four kinds of ownership.

- ***The beneficiary's parent.*** The beneficiary's parent who regularly transports him or her could be the registered owner. If the vehicle is adapted, one possible benefit might be a reduction in the high sales tax and annual personal property taxes that some states impose. The trust should have the ability to protect its financial interest if the vehicle is damaged or sold. This is typically done by calling the payment a loan and having the parent sign a promissory note for the value of the loan. The loan is then noted on the vehicle's title and recorded with the state's registry of motor vehicles. Your attorney can prepare the documents and explain how to record the loan.

- ***The beneficiary's relative.*** If the beneficiary lives with a relative such as a grandparent or sibling who will be driving the vehicle, that person could be the legal owner. However, there would probably not be any waiver of the sales or personal property taxes. In order to protect the trust's financial interest, there should be a written loan agreement and a reference to the agreement that is recorded with the state's registry of motor vehicles. (See discussion of the beneficiary's parent as the owner.)

- ***The beneficiary.*** Another option is to have the beneficiary own the vehicle. This might save sales and excise taxes in states that waive those taxes if the owner has a disability. However, the beneficiary's age is a consideration. If the beneficiary is a minor child (under age 18), he or she might not have the legal ability to own property or to sign the documents required to register, finance, or sell the vehicle.

  If the beneficiary is an adult, the person should be able to understand the significance of signing any legal documents needed to buy, sell, register, or insure the vehicle. However, if the person lacks capacity and is under guardianship, the legal guardian could own the vehicle.

  Another consideration when the beneficiary is the legal owner is the person's public benefits. Most public benefit programs allow a recipient to own a vehicle for his or her personal use. However, some states may place limits on the vehicle's value. Your attorney can tell you if this is the case in your state.

  You should also consider whether the Medicaid agency in your state would object to the beneficiary owning the vehicle. At least one state (Maryland) requires that a vehicle purchased with assets from a self-funded trust be owned by the trust, not the beneficiary.

- ***The special needs trust.*** Having the special needs trust own the vehicle is another option. However, some trustees report difficulties obtaining insurance when the trust is the owner. Also, some advisers recommend against having the special needs trust own the vehicle because the trust could be exposed to liability if there is an accident and the insurance is not sufficient to cover the loss.

Medical Costs

Some people with disabilities have significant medical needs. Fortunately, in most states, people with disabilities can obtain Medicaid insurance. The number of services that Medicaid will cover varies from state to state. You may be asked to use the trust funds to pay for the beneficiary's medical expenses.

There should not be any problem with SSI if you pay the beneficiary's medical expenses from the trust funds. The program rules allow an SSI recipient to get outside help with medical costs without affecting the SSI benefit.

For some Medicaid recipients, there can be a problem finding a medical provider that accepts Medicaid. For example, many private dentists do not accept Medicaid insurance because of the low reimbursement rates. As a result, some Medicaid recipients are accustomed to paying for dental care out of their personal funds. Some Medicaid recipients may choose to pay for a doctor privately, even though a Medicaid-insured physician is available. This could be the case if there is a longstanding relationship with a doctor who does not accept Medicaid. It is appropriate for you to use the trust funds to pay for these kinds of care.

What if the beneficiary does not have Medicaid? In that case, you can use the trust funds to pay for items like medical insurance premiums, co-payments, deductibles, and other out of pocket medical costs. These payments will not reduce the SSI benefit.

When Not to Pay for Medical or Transportation Costs

This chapter has focused on how you can assist the beneficiary by paying for his or her medical and transportation expenses. However, when the beneficiary needs medical and transportation items in order to work, it may not be desirable to pay for such costs. If that is the case, it is usually preferable for the person to pay for these items from his or her own funds (if he or she can afford to do so). That way, the person's SSI or SSDI benefit can be maximized. To grasp how this works, you need to understand how the SSI and SSDI programs consider a person's earnings. These rules are explained in Chapter 3, "SSI," and Chapter 4, "SSDI, Medicare, and Medicaid." We will summarize them again here.

Both the SSI and SSDI programs pay benefits to people who are unable to work and support themselves. With SSI, as a person's earnings go up, the SSI benefit goes down and may disappear altogether if the earnings are too high. Likewise, an SSDI recipient may lose his or her benefit when the earnings are too high. With SSDI, however, the monthly benefit is not reduced — it is completely eliminated if the person earns more than the program limit. (In 2010, that limit is $1,000 per month if the person does not qualify for so-called work incentives.) However, if an SSI or SSDI recipient has certain work-related expenses, these expenses can be deducted from the person's income. That way, earnings are reduced, and the SSI or SSDI benefit can be maximized.

There are many different kinds of work-related expenses. For example, a person might need an attendant to help with bathing and dressing before work. A person might incur transportation expenses for items like modifications to a vehicle, reimbursement for gas and related expenses for the person's vehicle, or driver assistance or taxicab fare if the person cannot use regular public transportation.

In order for an item to be deducted from the person's earnings, the person must pay for the item with his or her own funds. In other words, the item cannot be paid for by any outside source, including the person's special needs trust. Thus, if the beneficiary has any deductible work-related medical or transportation expenses, you should *not* pay for them from the trust funds. Instead, if possible, the beneficiary should pay for those expenses from his or her earnings. This will maximize the recipient's benefit.

CHAPTER 7
Housing

Finding decent, affordable housing can be challenging for people with disabilities who have low income. Yet many people with disabilities live independently in apartments, and some even own their own homes. Other people with disabilities live in housing that has been purchased by their families either individually or with other families of people with disabilities. Part I of this chapter covers housing, public benefits, and the special needs trust. Part II covers federal housing subsidies, including the Section 8 program, and explains how the special needs trust may affect a person's housing subsidy.

Part I – Housing and SSI

An SSI recipient is supposed to pay for all of his or her housing expenses out of the monthly SSI benefit. At least that is the theory. In reality, given the high cost of housing, many recipients receive outside assistance to pay for items like rent and utilities. However, in most states, a recipient's SSI benefit will be reduced if anyone (including the person's special needs trust) pays for his or her housing costs. Most, but not all, housing-related items are considered to be "in-kind income." (In-kind income is explained in Chapter 3, "SSI.") If an SSI recipient receives any in-kind income, the monthly benefit may be reduced by up to $244 (in 2010). The formula Social Security uses to calculate the reduction is explained later in Part I of this Chapter.

If the beneficiary receives SSDI (Social Security Disability Insurance), the benefit will not be reduced if the person receives assistance with housing costs, because the SSDI program does not consider in-kind income.

Housing Items the SSI Program Counts

Social Security considers the following items to be "countable" housing expenses that will reduce the SSI benefit:

- mortgage (principal and interest)
- rent
- real estate taxes
- heating fuel
- gas
- electricity
- water
- sewer
- garbage removal
- homeowner's insurance (if required by a lender)
- condominium charges that include any of the above items

[24 C.F.R. § 416.1130(b); POMS SI 00835.465D]

Housing Items the SSI Program Disregards

The Social Security Administration has not specifically stated which housing-related expenses are not countable. However, most advocates agree that SSI will not be reduced if you pay for any of the following items:

- telephone
- cable television
- premiums for personal property insurance
- paper products
- laundry and cleaning supplies
- cleaning and maintenance
- staff salaries (for example, support staff in a residence)
- repairs (plumbing, electrical, etc.) to a home the recipient owns
- furniture and furnishings
- capital improvements to the recipient's home (new roof, furnace, ramp, etc.)

How the Reduction in Benefits is Calculated

If the trustee pays for a countable housing item in any month, Social Security uses a complicated formula to calculate the reduction in SSI. The monthly benefit will be reduced by the lesser of the item's actual value or one-third of the federal benefit amount, plus $20. In 2010, the maximum reduction is $244. To do the calculation, divide the monthly SSI benefit of $674 by one-third to arrive at $224, then add $20 to arrive at $244. This rule (the Presumed Maximum Value Rule) is also covered in Chapter 3, "SSI."

> John, an SSI recipient, lives in his own apartment. In one month, John's family pays his $250 heating oil bill. That month, John's SSI will be reduced by $244.
>
> The next month, instead of paying for heating oil, John's family pays his $40 electric bill. That month, John's SSI payment will be reduced by $40.

Even if an SSI recipient receives more than one countable housing item in a month, SSI is never reduced by more than $244 per month (in 2010). This can be important for homeowners if the trustee must pay for the mortgage, real estate taxes, homeowner's insurance, and utilities every month.

If the trustee pays for a countable housing expense, it only affects the SSI benefit for one month, which is the month the benefit is received. The SSI benefit for the next month will not be affected.

Free Rent

Perhaps an SSI recipient lives apart from his or her family and does not pay any rent. An example would be a person who lives in a property his or her family owns. If the person receives free rent, the SSI benefit will be reduced by up to $244 per month (in 2010). The reduction will be less if the recipient can show that the actual value of the free rent is less than $244. [SI 00835.370]

Reduced Rent

Instead of living rent-free, some SSI recipients pay reduced rent. For purposes of the SSI program, reduced rent means rent that is less than the market rent the landlord could collect from another tenant. If an SSI recipient receives reduced rent, the SSI benefit would be reduced. This will occur if:

- The recipient is the parent or child of the landlord or the landlord's spouse, and
- The amount of rent the tenant is required to pay is less than the market rent.

The SSI benefit is reduced due to "in kind" income. The amount of in-kind income is the difference between the market rent and the amount of rent the tenant is required to pay or $244, whichever is less.[15] [SI 00835.380]

> Fred lives in an apartment owned by his father. The market rent is $750 per month, but Fred only pays $250. Fred has in-kind income of $500. His SSI benefit is reduced by $244 per month (in 2010).

Note that there are different rules in seven states: Illinois, Indiana, Wisconsin, New York, Connecticut, Vermont, and Texas. In those states, SSI will not be reduced if the tenant pays $244 or more (in 2010). However, if the tenant pays less than $244, SSI will be reduced by the difference between $244 and the actual rental amount. [20 C.F.R.§416.1130(b); SI00835.380] In the above example, if Fred lived in one of the seven states, his SSI benefit would not be reduced because his $250 rental payment is more than $244.

[15] $244 is one-third of the federal benefit amount ($674) plus $20 (in 2010).

Assisting the Beneficiary who Rents an Apartment

If the beneficiary rents an apartment, you, as trustee, should try to avoid paying for any countable housing expenses like rent, electricity, gas, heating fuel, or garbage removal. Instead, you can pay for non-countable housing expenses such as telephone, cable television, premiums for personal property (tenant) insurance, and non-food staples such as paper products, laundry supplies, and cleaning items. You can also pay salaries for residential support staff without affecting the SSI benefit.

> John, who receives SSI, lives in his own apartment with a roommate without a disability who receives a stipend for assisting John. If the trustee pays monthly rent of $450 to the landlord, John's monthly payment will be reduced by $244 (in 2010). However, if John uses his SSI funds to pay his rent and the trustee pays the stipend to the roommate, John's SSI benefit will not be reduced, because the trustee has not paid for a countable housing item.

Note that if paying rent to the landlord is a bad idea, giving John money to pay his landlord is a worse idea. As we explain throughout this book, if you give more than $20 in cash to the beneficiary in any month, SSI will be reduced on a dollar-for-dollar basis.

Assisting the Beneficiary who Owns His or Her Home

An SSI recipient may own his or her own home. A home is a non-countable resource, regardless of its value. [20 C.F.R. 416.1210; SI01130.100]

If the beneficiary owns his or her own home, you should try to avoid paying for any of the countable housing items listed earlier in this chapter (mortgage, real estate taxes, homeowner's insurance, utilities, heating fuel, water, sewer, garbage removal, or condominium charges that include any of these items). Of course, this may not be possible if the beneficiary has only limited income and must rely on the trust fund to pay for his or her housing costs. In that case, it is preferable for the beneficiary to incur a reduction in SSI rather than live in sub-standard housing or even risk losing his or her home.

There are several housing-related expenses that you can safely pay without affecting the SSI benefit. As is the case with the tenant who rents, you can pay for landscaping, snow removal, pest extermination, carpets, telephone, cable television, and non-food items such as paper products, laundry supplies, cleaning items, dishes, and cooking utensils. Salaries of residential support staff are also permitted expenditures. You can also pay for a new roof, construct an addition, make a bathroom accessible, and perform other repairs and improvements without affecting the SSI benefit.

Assisting the Beneficiary who Lives in a Home Owned by the Trust

An SSI recipient's benefit will not be affected if his or her special needs trust owns the home where he or she lives. Social Security does not presume that the person has any "free rent" that would reduce the monthly benefit. [SI01120.200F]

But owning a home can be an expensive proposition. The SSI recipient probably cannot afford to pay the housing costs like real estate taxes, homeowner's insurance, and maintenance. As a result, you — the trustee — must pay them. However, if you pay for countable housing costs from the trust funds in any month, SSI will be reduced by up to one-third of the monthly payment plus $20. (This amounts to $244 in 2010). [SI 01120F3c] Still, most trustees would probably agree that it is worthwhile to incur a reduction in SSI benefits in order to provide the beneficiary with a stable living arrangement.

Annual Housing Costs are Calculated Monthly

Some trustees think they can avoid a monthly reduction in SSI by paying large housing costs annually. For example, perhaps annual real estate taxes of $3,600 are billed quarterly ($900 every three months). The trustee thinks that if the taxes are paid annually, SSI might only be reduced one time per year.

This approach will not work because Social Security converts any housing bills to monthly amounts, even if the bills are paid less frequently. [20 C.F.R. §416.1133(c); SI 00835.474]

> For example, if an SSI recipient has annual real estate taxes of $3,600, those taxes are divided by the number of months in the billing period, resulting in monthly taxes of $300. Social Security charges the SSI recipient with in-kind income of $300 per month.

Co-ownership by a Family Member and the Special Needs Trust

A special needs trust and an individual such as a family member can own a residence together. This could occur if both contribute to purchase, renovate, or maintain the property. In this case, the deed must be carefully drafted to reflect the ownership interests. There should also be a written agreement that reflects the owners' respective financial responsibilities to pay bills and maintain the property. The agreement should say what would happen if the beneficiary wants to move to a different residence, or if one owner wants to sell the property and receive his or her share of the equity, or if an owner does not make the required payments.

Part II –Housing Subsidies

Many people with disabilities rely on public housing programs to keep a roof over their heads. Some people with disabilities live in low-cost rental apartments in public housing projects. Others live in private rental housing for which the state or federal government pays a portion of their rent. This section discusses federal housing subsidies, including the Section 8 program. We also explain how having a special needs trust can affect a person's eligibility and monthly rent.

Learn Whether Federal or State Rules Apply

Most subsidized housing programs are underwritten by the federal government. They are managed at the national level by the Department of Housing and Urban Development (HUD) and at the local level by Public Housing Authorities (PHAs).

Many states also have their own housing subsidy programs that are governed by their own state's rules. If you are a trustee managing a special needs trust for a person who has a housing subsidy, you must find out whether the program follows federal rules or state rules. There can be important differences among the programs.

For example, let's say you spend the trust funds on an item like a car or wheelchair. If the program follows the federal rules, the person's rent would probably not be affected. However, under a state program, the payment might be considered income that would cause the tenant's rent to increase. For instance, under the Massachusetts state-funded housing program, any funds the person receives from a trust are considered to be income. The public housing authority that manages the program can tell you which set of rules apply and explain its practices and procedures. In this book, we only cover federal housing rules because there is so much variation among the state rules.

The Importance of "Income"

Eligibility for federal public housing is primarily based on income. There is no asset limit. However, as we explain later, interest and dividends generated by a person's assets can sometimes be considered to be income. A person's income affects the housing benefit in two ways:

- A person must have a low income in order to qualify. Low income means 50% or less of the median income for the area. [42 U.S.C. §1437a(b)(2)]

- A person pays rent based on a percentage of his or her annual adjusted income. Most tenants pay about 30% of their adjusted income as rent. (Adjusted income is explained later in this chapter.)

In some cases, the funds you distribute from the special needs trust will be considered to be "income" that could cause the person to lose eligibility or significantly increase his or her rent. For that reason, it is important to understand how the PHA will consider the different kinds of payments you might make from the trust.

Working with the Public Housing Authority

A good practice is to set-up a meeting with the beneficiary and his or her worker at the PHA. The worker can explain how the PHA would consider items like regular distributions to help the beneficiary pay rent or utilities, or occasional distributions to buy a car or furniture. The worker can tell you if the PHA would consider these items to be "income" that would affect the tenant's eligibility or monthly rent.

Income the Public Housing Authority Counts

Federal housing programs use a uniform definition of income. (See 24 C.F.R. §5.609 located in the Appendix.) The definition of annual income is quite broad. It includes all amounts, monetary and non-monetary, that go to the tenant and members of the public housing household. It also includes amounts that the household members can be expected to receive from an outside source in the next 12 months following admission to the program or the annual review. [24 C.F.C.§5.609(a)]

Some of the items are:

- The full amount (before payroll deductions) of earnings from employment and self-employment.

- Interest, dividends, and other net income from any real or personal property the person owns.

- Periodic amounts received from Social Security, annuities, insurance policies, retirement funds, pensions, disability, or death benefits.

- Payments that replace earnings, such as unemployment and disability compensation.

- Welfare assistance.

- Alimony and child support.

- Regular gifts and contributions from an outside source, including persons not residing with the family. (Although the rule does not specifically say so, most authorities interpret this to include distributions from a special needs trust. Payments from a special needs trust are discussed later in this chapter.)

- Earnings (such as interest and dividends) generated by "family assets." Family assets include items like savings accounts, stocks, bonds, and investment real estate. If total family assets are $5,000 or less, any income produced by those assets is disregarded. However, if total family assets exceed $5,000, any income will be counted. HUD uses the greater of actual earnings or the "passbook rate" as set by HUD. [24 C.F.R.§ 609(b)(3)] In 2010, the passbook rate is less than one percent.

If a participant in a federal housing program transfers an asset for less than its fair value, then for two years after the transfer, HUD will treat the asset as if the participant still owned it and will assume the asset earns interest at the passbook rate. [24 C.F.R. 5.603(b)(3)]

A special needs trust is not considered to be a "family asset" (see the last bullet point) if the trust is irrevocable and not under the control of a member of the beneficiary's public housing household. [24 C.F.R.§5.603(b)(2)] (This can be a reason to have an independent trustee.) Any earnings that are generated by the special needs trust are not considered to be income. However, if you spend any of the trust funds, the expenditures could be considered income to the tenant/ beneficiary. (This is explained in the section titled "The Special Needs Trust and Federal Housing Subsidies" later in this chapter.)

> John, a subsidized tenant, inherits $100,000 and places it in a special needs trust. For the next two years, the housing authority will assume that John has interest income on $100,000 at the passbook rate. (After two years, the housing authority will not count the interest earned by the special needs trust.)

Income the Public Housing Authority does not Count

The items the PHA does not count when determining annual income include:

- Income from the employment of children under age 18.
- Payments received for foster care children.
- Lump sum additions to family assets, such as inheritances, insurance payments (including payments under health and accident insurance and worker's compensation), capital gains, and settlements for personal property losses.
- Any amounts received by the family specifically for, or as reimbursement of, medical expenses for any family member.
- Student financial assistance.
- Amounts received by an SSI recipient that are disregarded as income by SSI because the beneficiary is in a PASS program (see Chapter 5, "SSI and Work").

- Income received from certain work training programs funded by HUD.

- Income of a live-in aide, such as Personal Care Attendant, who provides necessary support services to a tenant with a disability.

- Temporary, nonrecurring, or sporadic income (including gifts).

[24 C.R.F. § 5.609(c) (reproduced in the Appendix)]

Last, as we mentioned earlier, any income earned by a special needs trust is excluded if the trust is irrevocable and the trustee is not a member of the beneficiary's public housing household.

Income and the Tenant's Share of the Rent

Under the federal subsidized housing rules, a tenant pays rent according to his or her "adjusted" annual income. Adjusted annual income means the tenant's gross income after certain mandatory deductions have been subtracted. These items are:

- $480 for each dependent.
- $400 for each family member who is age 62 or older or has a disability.
- Reasonable child care expenses necessary to enable a family member to work, look for work, or attend school.

Also, the sum of the following items is deducted to the extent they exceed 3% of the person's annual income:

- Unreimbursed medical expenses for any family member who is age 62 or older or has a disability.

- Unreimbursed reasonable attendant and equipment items (such as a wheelchair or walker) for each member of the family with a disability who needs the item in order to work.

After the tenant's adjusted income is determined, he or she pays 30 percent of that amount as rent, and the housing authority pays the balance of the rent directly to the landlord.

> Alex, whose adjusted income (see above definition) is $1,200 per month, is approved for a one-bedroom apartment that costs $900 per month. Alex pays the landlord $360 per month ($1,200 x 30% = $360), and the housing authority pays the landlord $540 per month.

The Special Needs Trust and Federal Housing Subsidies

As we explained earlier in this chapter, any funds held in a special needs trust are specifically excluded from the definition of family assets, provided that the trust is irrevocable and the trustee is not a member of the tenant's public housing household. Accordingly, any interest and dividend income earned by the trust is disregarded.

However, if you spend any of the trust funds, the amounts you spend will in some cases be considered to be "income" to the tenant that could affect his or her eligibility or increase the monthly rent. In general, whether the PHA will consider the payment to be income depends on two factors:

- The kind of expenses you pay.
- Whether the payments are regular or sporadic.

Note that unlike the SSI program, it does not matter whether you give the funds directly to the beneficiary or use them to pay his or her bills.

Items you Can Safely Pay For

Any funds you spend for the beneficiary's uninsured medical expenses are not considered to be income. This is true even if you pay the bills regularly (for example, you pay the beneficiary's monthly medical insurance premiums). Also, it doesn't matter if you give the beneficiary the funds to pay the bills, as long as they are spent on medical costs.

You can also make occasional distributions for items like education courses, a vacation, an automobile, furniture, a health club membership, or holiday gifts. There should not be a problem as long as the payments do not occur on a regular basis. The Section 8 program rules do not define what is meant by a "regular expense." However, the staff at the PHA that manages the beneficiary's program will probably tell you its practices if you ask.

Items you Should Avoid Paying For

If the payment is recurring, the PHA can count it as income. Thus, you should avoid making any regular payments from the trust. This would include giving the beneficiary a monthly allowance or paying his or her rent or utility bills. As a practical matter, however, it may not be possible to avoid making these kinds of payments if the beneficiary must rely on the trust fund for his or her living expenses.

The Section 8 Program

Throughout the United States, an important source of decent, safe, and affordable housing for low-income people with disabilities is the so-called Section 8 Program.[16] Section 8 is funded by the federal government and managed by the local PHAs, which provide rental vouchers

[16] The formal name is the Housing Choice Voucher Program (HCVP).

to qualified persons.[17] The Section 8 program follows the federal housing rules we explained earlier in Part II of this chapter.

The Section 8 Benefit

A Section 8 arrangement involves a three-party agreement among the tenant, the PHA, and a participating landlord who owns private rental housing. The tenant pays a portion of his adjusted income (30 percent in most cases), and the PHA pays the remaining rent (the voucher amount) directly to the landlord.

Section 8 vouchers can be either "mobile" or "project-based." Mobile vouchers belong to the tenant, so the tenant can take the voucher to a new apartment if he or she moves. Project-based vouchers are attached to the apartment and do not move with the tenant.

Maximum Rent the Landlord can Charge

The maximum rent a landlord can charge for any particular unit is set by the local PHA using certain "payment standards." These payment standards, which reflect modestly priced rental units in the local area, correspond to the number of bedrooms in the unit. Each PHA has a payment standard for a studio apartment, a one-bedroom unit, a two-bedroom unit, and so forth. The rent charged by the landlord cannot exceed the payment standard for the unit's size.

These payment standards are based on HUD's Fair Market Rents that are established annually for every housing market in the country. Not surprisingly, given the diverse housing markets within most states, there can be a relatively wide range of Fair Market Rents. In Massachu-

[17] There are currently four types of housing assistance provided by the Section 8 program: tenant-based rental assistance, project-based rental assistance, home-ownership assistance, and down payment assistance. This section discusses only the tenant-based rental assistance portion of the program, because the vast majority of Section 8 participants use that program. For more information on all four parts of the Section 8 program, see "Section 8 Made Simple," published by the Technical Assistance Collaborative, Inc., listed in Chapter 16, "Resources."

setts, for example, in 2010, the Fair Market Rent for a one-bedroom apartment was $1,156 in Boston, $726 in Springfield, and $681 in Pittsfield. (Springfield and Pittsfield are smaller cities than Boston and are located about two and four hours, respectively, from Boston.) The 2010 Fair Market Rents for all fifty states and the District of Columbia can be obtained from the HUD website (see Chapter 16, "Resources") or from any PHA office.

Once the PHA sets its annual payment standards, they are not set in stone. The PHA has some flexibility to approve a higher payment standard, on a case by case basis, as a reasonable accommodation for a person with a disability. [24 C.F.R. § 982.505(d)] For example, the PHA could approve a fully accessible apartment that costs more than a non-accessible unit for a person who needs that kind of accommodation.

Maximum Rent the Tenant Can Pay

The rules allow a tenant to choose an apartment that costs more than the payment standard for a comparable apartment in the area. In that case, however, the PHA will only pay the difference between 30 percent of the tenant's income and the applicable payment standard. Thus, in addition to paying 30 percent of his or her income for rent, the tenant must also pay the difference between the payment standard and the actual rent.

> Matt has income of $1,400 per month. The payment standard for an apartment in Matt's area is $900 per month, but he chooses an apartment that costs $1,000 per month. Matt pays $420 (30% of his income) to his landlord, and the housing authority pays the landlord $480 ($900 - $420 = $480). Matt must pay the additional $100 of rent from his own funds.

The tenant's right to choose a more expensive apartment is not unlimited. According to the Section 8 program rules, in most cases a tenant cannot pay more than 40 percent of his or her income toward rent.

Thus, in the above example, the PHA would not approve an apartment that cost $1,200 per month, because then Matt's share of the rent would amount to $720, which is 51 percent of his income. There is an exception to the 40 percent rule for existing Section 8 tenants where the landlord increases the rent (with the permission of the PHA). In that case, the PHA might approve a higher tenant payment as long as the rent charged by the landlord is reasonable, as determined by the PHA.

Can a Family Member of the Tenant be the Section 8 Landlord?

Some families would like to rent an apartment in their home (such as a unit in a duplex or a so-called in-law apartment in a single family home) to a relative with a disability. That way, the relative is close by, and the family can provide care and supervision. Many PHAs do not permit this kind of arrangement because according to the rules, the owner may not be the parent, child, grandparent, grandchild, sister, or brother of any member of the tenant's family. However, there are two instances where the owner may be a close family member:

- Reasonable accommodation. The PHA must permit the arrangement if it is needed as a "reasonable accommodation" for the family member with a disability. [24 C.F.R. § 982.306(d)] The regulations do not give any examples of a "reasonable accommodation." Some advocates suggest that a duplex or in-law type apartment might qualify if the family member needs 24-hour supervision and the other family members will provide the supervision.

- Arrangements that have existed prior to 1999. If the family rental arrangement has been in existence since before April 1999, the PHA must approve it. (That is when the law that prohibits family rental arrangements took effect.)

Can the Trustee be the Section 8 Landlord?

If the trust owns the beneficiary's residence, you can apply to be the Section 8 landlord. However, the PHA might not approve your application if you are a close family member of the beneficiary. As we explained above, the PHA will not allow the tenant's parent, child, grandparent, grandchild, sister, or brother to be the landlord, unless that is needed as a reasonable accommodation.

Some PHAs take the position that the trustee cannot be the landlord if he or she is one of these family members. We think this is wrong, because a special needs trust is a separate legal entity that should not be subject to these family-landlord-tenant restrictions. We would also argue that although the trustee may happen to be related to the tenant, he or she has a separate legal status and duties that are governed by the trust document. Fortunately, many PHAs agree with our position. If your PHA does not agree, you can appeal the decision and ask that a reasonable accommodation be made.

A Section 8 arrangement involving a trust as the landlord can be quite complicated to manage. However, if it is successful, it can provide a significant economic benefit to the beneficiary and the trust.

Briefly, it works this way. The beneficiary, as the tenant, obtains a housing subsidy from his or her local PHA. The trustee, as the landlord, agrees to participate in the housing subsidy program and signs a written lease with the beneficiary and the PHA. The beneficiary pays 30 percent of his or her income to the trustee as rent, and the PHA pays the remaining rent to the trustee.

This arrangement helps the beneficiary by reducing his or her monthly rent. The trust also benefits from an increased income stream.

A New Trend in Housing

We have come a long way from the time when people with disabilities were routinely institutionalized. Fortunately, for the most part, the institution is a relic of the past. Now the trend is to integrate people with disabilities into all aspects of community life, including housing. We wholeheartedly endorse this practice. But housing is expensive, and the states do not provide a community residence for everyone who wants one.

Some parents who have the financial means to do so are forming partnerships with one another and the state to provide community housing for their children with disabilities. For example, two or more families might pool their resources to purchase a home and maintain it by paying the mortgage, real estate taxes, insurance, repairs, etc. The state hires a private non-profit agency to provide the support staff. When the parents are deceased, the funds in a son's or daughter's special needs trust can keep the arrangement going. You (the trustee) may have the chance to participate in one of these partnerships — and you might even have the opportunity to set one up. However, these partnerships can be complicated and expensive, and you probably can't proceed without the blessing — and financial backing — of the state. But, if they are successful, these arrangements can provide comfortable, stable housing for a person with a disability.

Chapter 8

The Trustee

This chapter covers several trustee matters, including appointments, resignations, trustee selection, and bonds. We also discuss how much compensation trustees may charge for their services.

Accepting the Trusteeship

Let's say the grantor has named you to be the trustee. How do you accept the office? If you signed the original trust document, you don't need to do anything else. You are already the trustee.

If you are named to be a successor trustee, you should review the trust document for instructions on how to accept the office. (A successor trustee serves after the previous trustee has left office.) Most trust documents require you to sign a written acceptance. A sample Acceptance of Trustee form is located in the Appendix. The original Acceptance should be kept with the trust records. You should give copies to the beneficiary or his or her representative, the grantor (if the person is still living), and any co-trustees.

Resigning from the Trust

What if you are serving as the trustee but no longer want to do so? Most trusts have a specific procedure for a trustee to resign. Typically this will require you to provide a written notice to the effect that you no longer want to remain in office. You should sign a Resignation form. A sample Resignation form is located in the Appendix. The Resignation should be given at least thirty days before you intend to leave office. After you sign the form, put the original Resignation with the other trust documents and give copies to the beneficiary (or his or her legal representative) and the individuals who have the right to appoint and remove trustees (if there are any).

Sometimes a court is supervising a trust. This could be the case if the trust was created as the result of a lawsuit and the court retained supervision over the trust. If the trust you are managing is supervised by a court, you may need to get the court's approval to resign. The court will probably not accept your resignation until you have filed your final financial account and a successor trustee is ready to take over.

Even if a court is not involved, you should not necessarily assume that you are "off the hook" simply because you have delivered the required Resignation. You will probably remain responsible for anything that happens to the trust property until a successor trustee takes possession of it. You will also remain liable for your actions during the time you served as the trustee. You should prepare a financial account and have all beneficiaries (the beneficiary with a disability and the remainder beneficiaries) approve it. Instructions to do so are located in the "Accounts" section of Chapter 10, "Everyday Management."

Removing the Trustee

What if the trustee is not doing a good job and must be removed? Most trusts describe the procedure to remove a trustee. For example, some trusts require court approval, while others simply authorize a third person to remove the trustee. Some trusts limit the number of times that trustees can be removed in any given period.

The standard for removing trustees can vary from trust to trust. Some trusts state that a trustee can only be removed for reasonable cause. Other trusts allow a trustee to be removed at any time and for any reason.

If the trust does not contain any particular standard for removing the trustee, then state law will apply. Your attorney can explain the standards in the state that govern the trust you are managing. Some states have passed the Uniform Trust Code. Under that law, the grantor, co-trustee, or beneficiary may ask the court to remove a trustee. The court may remove a trustee if:

- The trustee has committed a serious breach of trust.

- There is a lack of cooperation among co-trustees that substantially impairs the administration of the trust.

- Removal of the trustee best serves the interests of the trust because of unfitness, unwillingness, or persistent failure of the trustee to administer the trust effectively.

- There has been a substantial change of circumstances or removal is requested by all the beneficiaries, and the court finds that removal of the trustee best serves the interests of all the beneficiaries; removal is consistent with a material (important) purpose of the trust; and a suitable co-trustee or successor trustee is available. [Uniform Trust Code, sec. 706]

Who Should be the Trustee?

The Beneficiary

The beneficiary with a disability should never be the trustee or co-trustee. This would defeat one of the major goals of the special needs trust, which is to prevent the trust from being counted as a resource for most government benefit programs. Most such programs preclude the beneficiary from having any direct or indirect control over the trust property. That is difficult, if not impossible, to show if the beneficiary is the trustee. Thus, if the trust document names the beneficiary to be the initial trustee, he or she should resign and make arrangements to have an alternate trustee appointed. If the beneficiary is named as a successor trustee, he or she should not accept the office.

The Beneficiary's Parents

Sometimes when a minor child with a disability has received compensation for an injury, the parents want to be the trustees. But parents are probably not the best choice. There are two reasons. One is the asset limitations of the public benefit programs the beneficiary or his or her family may participate in. The other reason has to do with potential family relationship issues.

If a minor child receives SSI, there could a problem if the parent is the trustee. Although the program rules do not specifically prohibit a parent from serving in this capacity, there is an implied restriction. If the beneficiary has any control over the trust funds, he or she cannot receive SSI. However, lack of control can be difficult to show if the trustee is the beneficiary's parent. After all, the parent is legally responsible for the minor child.

In addition, there could be a problem with SSI if the parent-trustee takes any money out of the trust. The reason has to do with the way Social Security considers income when there is a minor child in the family who receives SSI. For purposes of financial eligibility, Social Security considers the parents' income and resources in addition to the child's income and resources. (This is explained in Chapter 3, "Supplemental Security Income.")

It is not unusual for the trustee to take money out of the trust to pay for items like the minor child's living expenses (his or her proportionate share of the rent, mortgage, real estate taxes, or utilities), medical care, or monthly loan payments for an adapted vehicle. In that case, Social Security may consider these withdrawals to be income to the family. Since the entire family's income is considered when there is a child recipient, that could reduce or eliminate SSI.

Similarly, if the family participates in the Temporary Assistance to Needy Families (TANF) program, there can be a problem if the parent is the trustee.[18] In most states, the trustee cannot be a person who is under the direction or control of any person who lives in the beneficiary's household. This would preclude the parent who is raising the child from being the trustee. The trust would be counted as a resource and the family could not get benefits. Your attorney can tell you if this is the case in your state.

Besides these public benefits issues, another problem with parents serving as the trustees can be conflicts of interest. Sometimes the

---

[18] TANF was enacted in 1996 as the successor program to Aid to Families with Dependent Children (AFDC). TANF is a federally funded basic support program that is managed by the states for poor families with children. In most cases, a TANF recipient cannot get benefits for more than five years. Most states have their own names for TANF. For example, in Massachusetts, it is called Transitional Aid to Families with Dependent Children (TAFDC). The program rules may be different in each state.

parent-trustee will use the minor beneficiary's funds in ways that benefit the entire family. For example, it is not unusual for the trust to pay for a family vacation, a residence where the entire family lives, or an adapted vehicle that everyone uses. What will happen when the child with a disability grows up and wants to move away from home? It may be difficult for a parent-trustee to sort out what is in the child's interest versus what is in the family's interest. The parent could even be exposed to charges — legitimate or not — that he or she has misused the funds. This problem could be compounded if the parent's paperwork is poor or non-existent.

An Independent Trustee

An independent trustee is often the solution to these public benefits and conflict of interest problems. An independent trustee is a person or organization that has no beneficial interest in the trust property. This means that the independent trustee can never be eligible to receive any trust property (other than his or her fee). Neither the beneficiary nor any member of his immediate family can qualify as an independent trustee.

Most problems with public benefits we described can be avoided if there is an independent trustee. An independent trustee may be able to avoid the conflicts of interest that can arise for a family trustee. An independent trustee may be in a much better position to distinguish between the family's needs and the beneficiary's needs. The person can also serve as an objective voice in a situation that can become emotionally charged.

A potential downside to using an independent trustee is the cost. An independent trustee will almost always charge a fee for his or her services, whereas a parent or sibling might not charge anything. On the other hand, an independent trustee may have investment experience that family members lack. Through proper investments, an independent trustee may be able to earn his or her fee, and the family may even come out ahead.

Surety Bonds

Some trusts require the trustee to provide a surety bond. A surety bond is insurance that protects the beneficiary if the trustee mismanages or misappropriates the trust property. Surety bonds are sold by insurance companies that offer this kind of coverage. Whether or not the trustee must provide a bond is usually stated in the trust document.

Some trusts excuse a trustee who is a relative of the beneficiary from giving bond but require a professional or corporate trustee to provide one. In this context, a professional trustee usually means an attorney, accountant, or other business professional who is not related by blood to the beneficiary. An example of a corporate trustee is a bank or a corporation such as a chapter of The Arc or a similar disability organization.

If you are a non-professional trustee, such as a family member, you will probably not be able to obtain a bond. We do not know of any insurance companies that will cover people who are managing a single trust. Thus, if the trust document requires you to provide a bond, you should try to get an exemption. Perhaps the beneficiaries or the people the trust document names to appoint and remove trustees (if there are any) would be willing to give you an exemption, if the trust terms allow them to do so.

If you are a professional person who is managing a trust, you might be able to get special coverage under your professional liability policy. For lawyers, most standard malpractice policies do not cover trust management activities. However, to be sure, tell your insurance agent about the trust and check your policy. If your policy does not cover trust management, you might be able to obtain separate coverage for this purpose. Alternatively, you could obtain a fidelity policy that specifically covers your trustee activities.

If you work for a professional trustee such as a bank, you probably will not have to do anything extra to obtain a bond. The institution will most likely have an insurance policy that provides coverage.

If the trust requires you to obtain a bond, who should for pay the premium? This point may be negotiated between you and the beneficiary (or his or her representative) and the remainder beneficiaries. If you already have coverage under an existing insurance policy, you should not charge anything for the bond. You can simply build the cost into your trustee fee. But if you must duplicate coverage that you already carry at your own expense, it may be appropriate to have the trust pay the premium.

Trustee Fees

Trustees sometimes ask whether they can charge a fee for their services. Some trust documents do not say anything about trustee fees. Still, a trustee can receive reasonable compensation for his or her services. This is a basic principle of trust law. Even if you choose to waive your fee, you will be held to the same standard of responsibility as a trustee who receives compensation. If you are careless or mismanage the trust, you could be liable to the trust for any loss.

Another point about trustee compensation is that it is taxable income to the recipient. You must report it on your federal, state, and local income tax returns.

How do Trustees Set Their Fees?

There is a wide variation in the fees that trustees charge. Sometimes trustee fees are paid according to a formula that is based on the amount of trust property. This is usually the case if the trustee is a professional or corporate trustee (bank, trust company, or law firm). If the trustee is an individual, the person is more likely to be compensated according to the services he or she actually performs. Occasionally the trust document will set the trustee's compensation at a fixed amount (for example, $3,000 per year). However, this arrangement is relatively rare.
Here are some key points about trustee fees:

- Professional and corporate trustees (banks, trust companies, and law firms)

  Most professional and corporate trustees use a formula that is based on the size of the trust and the amount of income it earns. The trustees receive a percentage of the trust assets under management and a percentage of the annual income. The following is a sample schedule that shows the annual fee a trustee might charge:

  1.0% of the trust's market value for amounts up to $500,000,
  plus
  0.8% of the trust's market value for amounts ranging from $500,001 to $1,000,000,
  plus
  0.3% of the trust's market value for amounts ranging from $1,000,001 to $5,000,000,
  plus
  0.1% of the trust's market value for amounts over $5,000.000,
  plus
  6.0% of the annual income earned.

What services are included when there is a fee schedule? These can vary among trustees. Most professional and corporate trustees handle the investment and accounting functions themselves, so there are not usually any charges for these services. However, if an outside investment advisor or an accountant is hired, their fees might be billed separately to the trust. A trustee might charge an additional fee if time has to be spent on SSI or other public benefit matters. And if the trustee is also providing any legal services to the beneficiary, the legal fees may be charged in addition to the trustee's normal fees.

As for the frequency of payment, most professional and corporate trustees bill quarterly or even monthly for their services.

- Individual trustees

Most individual trustees charge a fee based on the services they perform. There is no set formula to arrive at the fee. Most trustees estimate how many hours may be needed to manage the trust over the course of a year, and then allocate a dollar value to those hours. In part, the dollar value will be set according to the trustee's abilities and experience. A trustee with a professional background (such as law or financial services) might charge $100 to $150 per hour. However, a trustee who does not have any professional skills might only charge $20 to $30 per hour. Note that these figures are only general illustrations. Your attorney can tell you the customary rates that trustees charge in your location.

Another factor used to determine compensation is the difficulty of any particular task. You would charge a higher rate for providing accounting services (or meeting with an accountant) than for making a bank deposit or balancing the checkbook. After the trustee has made a general estimate of the time required, he or she might decide on a flat rate for the year. Alternatively, the trustee might charge an hourly rate. The fee could be paid one time a year or more frequently, such as every three months.

If there is an individual trustee, the trust will usually pay separately for any additional costs such as accounting, tax preparation, and attorney's services. However, the trustee might include these costs in his or her fee. You can also receive reimbursement for any out-of-pocket costs, such as postage, long distance telephone charges, and travel costs (mileage, tolls, etc.). A trustee who is a professional person such as an attorney would probably also charge separately for any services he or she provides to the beneficiary in non-trust matters. These could include guardianship services, representation in Social Security matters, or appeals within public agencies that provide housing or medical benefits.

When it comes to setting a fee, here are some factors that should be taken into account:

» *The trustee's skill and experience.* A professional person such as an attorney or financial planner is generally entitled to more compensation than a person who has no specific skills or knowledge of trust law and practices. A professional may work more efficiently and expend less time. A professional is also less likely to require outside assistance, which the trust might have to pay for if the trustee is a non-professional.

» *The time devoted to trust duties.* Some trusts only require a few hours each month to manage, while others are more time-consuming. Consider the amount of time you spend on tasks like managing the books and records, monitoring investments, preparing income tax returns or working with a tax preparer, visiting the beneficiary and responding to requests for payments, making payments, preparing financial accounts and providing them to the beneficiaries, and preparing reports and responding to requests for information from agencies that provide assistance to the beneficiary, such as Social Security and public housing.

» *The amount of trust property.* In general, the larger the trust, the more compensation the trustee will receive. Most trustees charge less to manage a small trust. This is the case even though some small trusts can be more complicated and time-consuming to manage than large trusts. If the trust is very small, you might have to charge a small fee in order to avoid exhausting the trust funds.

- *The kind of trust property.* A trust that contains traditional investments (such as cash, stocks, and bonds) is often easier to manage than one that contains a multi-unit rental property.

- *The degree of difficulty, responsibility, and risk involved in managing the trust.* If the beneficiary receives SSI, your job may be harder than if he or she receives SSDI. With SSI, you must be careful that the funds you spend from the trust will not reduce or eliminate the beneficiary's SSI stipend. In addition, liability could be an issue if the trust contains property like the beneficiary's home or investment real estate. You could be exposed to significant liability if you fail to properly monitor the investment or keep the property insured.

- *The fees other trustees with similar skills and experience charge in the trustee's community.* You can charge a fee that is equivalent to what others with comparable experience charge in the part of the state where you live or work. A trustee in a large metropolitan area can sometimes charge a larger fee than one in a rural area.

- *The nature and costs of services provided by others.* The overall administrative costs — including your fees — must be reasonable in relation to the size of the trust. If you are not a professional person, you might have to hire outside help for items like bookkeeping, accounting, investment advice, and tax services. In setting your fee, you must consider the cost of this outside help. One reason professional trustees charge more than individual trustees is that they can perform these services themselves or have them performed "in-house" at a reduced cost. You might have to reduce your fee if the trust is paying separately for most or all outside services.

- *The quality of your performance.* A conscientious, frugal trustee who is attentive to the beneficiary's needs may deserve more compensation than a trustee who is lax and neglects his or her duties. If your neglect costs the trust money (for example, you pay the income taxes late and interest and penalties are imposed), you may have to decrease your fee that year, or at least not look for an increase the following year.

Pay Yourself Regularly in Order to Avoid Potential Problems when the Trust Ends

If you are an individual trustee, it is important to pay yourself regularly. This means compensating yourself at least annually, if not more frequently. This will prevent any potential problems with the beneficiary's relatives or the state Medicaid agency when the trust ends. In our experience, some trustees are reluctant to pay themselves anything while the beneficiary is alive. This is especially true if the trustee is a relative of the beneficiary. These trustees are uncomfortable taking money from a family member with a disability who might need the money in the future. Their plan is to pay themselves after the beneficiary has died, if there are sufficient funds left in the trust to do so.

This way of thinking may cause you substantial problems in getting paid when the trust ends. One possible difficulty could come from the remainder beneficiaries. (These are the individuals — usually members of the beneficiary's family, and sometimes charities — who will receive the remaining trust funds when the beneficiary dies and the trust ends.) For example, suppose you have not paid yourself anything while the beneficiary was alive. When the beneficiary dies and it is time to close the trust, you pay yourself for ten years of trustee services. The remainder beneficiaries might balk at approving your fee. They could argue that you have waived any compensation. However, as long as your rate of payment is reasonable and you actually performed the services listed on your bill, you will most likely prevail. A basic principal of trust law is that a trustee is entitled to be paid — even belatedly — for his or her services.

A better strategy is to avoid putting yourself in a position where your fee can be challenged. You should pay yourself regularly and also include your fee on the annual financial accounts you provide to the beneficiaries. (A description of the trust accounting procedures is contained in Chapter 10, "Everyday Management.") When the trust ends, the remainder beneficiaries will not be able to challenge your fee, because you have already disclosed it.

If you defer paying yourself, you might also face a significant problem with the state Medicaid agency. You might be dealing with that agency if the trust contains a so-called Medicaid payback provision. (In some special needs trusts, any assets that remain in the trust when the beneficiary dies must be used to reimburse the state for the Medicaid services the person received while he or she was alive.) In that case, the state Medicaid agency may assert a claim on the trust assets for the total cost of the beneficiary's Medicaid covered expenses. If the Medicaid claim is more than the remaining trust assets, the state's claim might have priority over your unpaid trustee's fee. That being the case, you might not receive anything for your services. The problem of Medicaid recovery and unpaid trustee fees is covered in Chapter 13, "Closing the Trust."

Chapter 9
Trustee Responsibilities

In order to properly manage a special needs trust, you must understand your basic responsibilities. These responsibilities may not be described anywhere in the trust document. This chapter will explain them. With responsibilities, come liabilities. If the trust suffers a loss as a result of your actions, the beneficiaries might try to hold you accountable. We suggest some steps you can take to protect yourself.

The Fiduciary Duty

In reading about trusts, you may encounter the term *fiduciary*. A trustee is one kind of fiduciary. A fiduciary is held to the highest standard of conduct. Managing someone else's property is different than managing your own funds. If you are handling someone else's property, you must be scrupulous. You must make sure the funds are properly invested and earn a reasonable rate of return. You must keep accurate and complete financial records of the property and periodically account to others for what you have done. You should never combine your own money with property you are managing for someone else, and you should never borrow from the trust fund.

Besides these general fiduciary standards, each state has its own rules that govern trusts. These may be based on laws that were passed by the legislature (statutory law) or rules that derive from specific court cases (case law). It is essential that you work with a local attorney who can explain the rules in your state.

Primary Responsibilities

Trustees must adhere to the primary responsibilities listed below. Your attorney can explain any specific requirements in your state.

Follow the Terms of the Trust

A trustee must carry out the grantor's intentions as they are expressed in the trust document. (The grantor is the person who set-up the trust.) It is essential to read the trust document carefully. How did the grantor want the trust property to be used? What guidelines, if any, did he or she provide concerning trust distributions? If the trust document does not contain any specific directions, the grantor may have left a "side letter" or "letter of intent" to guide you.

Some trust documents contain contradictory instructions. For example, the trustee may be directed to "supplement but not supplant public benefits" and also to "use the trust property in ways that will best help the beneficiary to lead a comfortable and fulfilling life," or words to that effect. Both goals may not be achievable. Let's say the beneficiary receives SSI and needs better housing. Let's also say that there are enough funds in the trust to pay for housing, but only at the cost of reducing the beneficiary's SSI payment. (As we explain throughout this book, the beneficiary's SSI award may be reduced if the trustee pays for housing costs.) How can you reconcile the conflicting instructions?

One way is to look outside the document and consider the circumstances that led the grantor to create the trust. If the grantor is the beneficiary's parent, the primary goal of the trust is almost always to provide for the beneficiary's, health, happiness, and well-being. No parent would want his or her son or daughter to live in substandard housing if a good alternative is available. You might be able to find adequate support for the decision to purchase comfortable housing — even if it causes a reduction in public benefits. These situations can be difficult. Whatever you decide to do, it is best to prepare written notes explaining why you did or did not take a particular course of action. Notes can be useful if you are ever questioned in the future about your actions.

Do Not Have any Personal Financial Dealings with the Trust

A trustee should never have any personal business transactions with the trust. These kinds of transactions are called "self-dealing." Self-dealing means that the trustee, acting in his or her fiduciary capacity, enters into a business arrangement with himself or herself in an individual capacity. You engage in self-dealing if you borrow money from the trust, lend money to the trust, lend trust assets to your family or friends, buy property from the trust, or sell property to the trust.

The basic rule is that you must not allow your personal interests to compete with the trust's or the beneficiary's interests. You cannot avoid this if you engage in a self-dealing transaction. Even if you have a good reason for the transaction, you should not proceed with the deal. This is true even if the proposed terms are by all objective standards fair, reasonable, and beneficial for the trust. Moreover, finding a neutral third party to represent the trust for purposes of the proposed transaction is not the answer. The only option is for you to resign and then go forward in your individual capacity. Even then, you could open yourself up to charges that you have abused your fiduciary position.

A widely recognized exception to the rule against self-dealing concerns payment of trustee fees. A trustee can take money from the trust assets to pay his or her fee. This inherent conflict is permissible because it would be unreasonable to expect a trustee to serve without compensation.

Keep the Beneficiary Informed

A trustee has a basic duty to keep the beneficiary informed about what he or she is doing with the trust property. This is true even if the beneficiary cannot understand the information you are providing. In that case, the information should be given to the beneficiary's legal representative. This could be the person's court-appointed guardian or conservator, or someone the beneficiary has designated to represent his or her interests.

One way to keep the beneficiary informed is to show the books and records of the trust if you are asked to do so. Another way to keep the beneficiary informed is to provide regular financial accounts. An account is a written summary of the financial activity of the trust for a specific period of time, usually a year. It shows the income the trust produces, the trust expenses, and how the property is invested. The accounting process is described in detail in Chapter 10, "Everyday Management."

Protect the Trust Property

A trust is not going to do the beneficiary much good if the money is lost, mismanaged, or stolen. The trust property must be protected, and it is your job to protect it. Make sure the funds are properly invested with a reputable bank or investment house. Keep all automobiles, real estate, and any other property the trust owns properly insured. Do not make any questionable loans, and never borrow money from the trust.

Keep the Trust Property Separate from other Property

All trust assets must be kept in a separate trust account. Never keep any trust property under your own name or in your own bank account. This is called co-mingling, and it is a violation of your fiduciary duty. If the beneficiary has any separate property, do not combine it with the trust property. This is true whether the beneficiary owns the property in his or her own name or you have legal title to it. (You might have legal ownership of the beneficiary's separate property if you are his or her legal guardian or representative for government benefits.)

Make the Trust Property Productive

A trustee has a duty to make the trust property productive. You should avoid keeping all the trust property in a no- or low-interest checking account. If the beneficiary does not need the funds from month to month, consider purchasing a certificate of deposit or investing in a money market, bond fund, or stock mutual fund. You can read about the different kinds of trust investments in the Appendix to Chapter 12, "Investment Basics."

Enforce Claims and Defend the Trust

A trustee should take reasonable steps to enforce claims of the trust. Perhaps someone fails to turn over property that belongs to the trust. Or maybe an insurance company wrongfully refuses to pay a claim. In that case, you could consider taking legal action. Before you bring a lawsuit, however, there are a number of factors to consider. These include the merits of the claim, the cost to pursue the lawsuit, and the likelihood that the trust will actually recover any losses. Even if you win, the person you sue may not have any resources to pay a judgment.

You also have a responsibility to defend claims that may be brought against the trust. In our experience, it is rare for a special needs trust to be sued. Nevertheless, if this did occur, you must investigate the claim to determine if it has any merit. If you believe the claim is baseless, you should reject it. One option might be to resolve the matter through mediation or arbitration. If court action appears inevitable, you should take into account the cost to defend the suit. In some situations, it may be more cost effective to settle the claim rather than risk an adverse result. Most trusts give the trustee authority to settle claims on behalf of the trust.

Use any Special Skills you Possess for the Benefit of the Trust

Perhaps you have special skills or expertise, such as a background in law or finance. If you do, you must use those skills in managing the trust. A professional person who is managing a trust is held to a higher standard of performance than a family member or someone who has no special abilities. If you are an attorney, you might be bound by the rules of professional conduct in your state. This could be the case even though you are not providing any legal services to the trust or the beneficiaries.

Pay Income Taxes When They are Due

When you invest the trust funds, they will probably generate income in the form of interest, dividends, and capital gains. As the trustee, it is your responsibility to make sure that the income is reported to the federal, state, and local governments in a timely manner. You are also responsible for making sure that any taxes are paid. If the taxes are not paid and the trust does not have sufficient funds to pay them, the government may look to you for payment. And if your mistake costs the trust interest and penalties, the beneficiaries may want you to personally make up the loss.

To meet your duty to pay the income taxes, you should carefully monitor the investments and collect all 1099 forms (statements of interest and dividends). You should hire a qualified tax preparer to assist you to file the returns and pay any taxes that may be owed. You should also pay any quarterly estimated taxes when they are due. Taxes are explained in Chapter 11, "Taxes."

Maintain the Beneficiary's Privacy

You should not disclose any information about the trust, including the amount of funds you are managing, unless it is necessary to do so. Naturally you will share this kind of information with the beneficiary and any government agencies that provide benefits to him or her. However, other individuals, such as the staff where the beneficiary lives, don't need to know how much money is in the trust. This is a private matter between you and the beneficiary and his or her legal representative.

Trustee Liability

If you make a mistake managing the trust, you could be personally responsible to make up the loss. Whether this will occur depends in part on what the trust document says about trustee liability. Many trusts contain an "exculpatory clause." This legal term is designed to protect the trustee. A common exculpatory clause states that if a trustee acts in good faith, the trustee will not be liable for any particular action he or she takes or fails to take. However, an exculpatory clause would probably not protect a trustee who acts in bad faith or with gross negligence. Also, an exculpatory clause would probably not protect you from any intentional act on your part that causes the trust to lose money. For example, you would be considered to have acted intentionally if you borrowed money from the trust and did not return it or loaned money to your friends who did not repay it.

If a trust does not include an exculpatory clause, the law of the state that governs the trust will apply. In many states, you can be personally liable for a *negligent* (careless) act that causes the trust to lose money. Some examples of negligent acts are filing income tax returns late so that interest and penalties are imposed, or allowing insurance to lapse so that there is an uninsured loss.

A particular concern for many trustees is investment losses. Trustees worry that if the trust loses money in any year, they may be personally liable to make up the loss. In our experience, trustees are rarely, if ever, personally responsible. Most states have a Prudent Investor Act that will protect you from any losses as long as you adhere to its standards. The Prudent Investor Act is explained in Chapter 12, "Investments." If the trust contains an exculpatory clause, it may also protect you.

Protecting Yourself

Given all these potential risks, what can you do to protect yourself? Your best approach is to do the best job you can. In summary, you should:

- Read the trust thoroughly and understand your responsibilities.

- Make sure that all property that is supposed to be part of the trust is actually registered to the trust.

- Keep all assets — real estate, automobiles, and any other property the trust owns — adequately insured.

- Pay income taxes in a timely manner.
- Keep the trust property separate from your own property.
- Keep detailed records of all trust activity and send periodic financial accounts — annually if not quarterly — to the beneficiary or his or her legal representative.
- Never borrow money from the trust or have any personal business dealings with the trust.
- Let the beneficiary know how you are investing and spending the trust funds.

If you have any questions about what you are supposed to be doing, don't hesitate to get advice from a qualified professional. There are suggestions for finding someone in Chapter 14, "Getting Help."

Chapter 10
Everyday Management

This chapter covers the practical aspects of managing a special needs trust. We tell you how to develop a budget, open a bank account, and create a filing system. We also explain your responsibilities to report to the beneficiaries from time to time about your financial activities. We also alert you to new Social Security guidelines that pertain to initial trust bank accounts for some self-funded trusts.

The Budget

As you take over managing the trust, you should create a budget. A budget will let you know how much you can afford to spend each year without depleting the trust fund.

How to Develop the Budget

You begin the process of developing a budget by assessing the beneficiary's needs. These will vary. A person who lives in a hospital-type setting may not need very much from the trust. A person who is active and lives relatively independently may need a substantial number of disbursements.

To find out what the beneficiary will need, meet with the person and others who know him or her. If you are taking over from a prior trustee, perhaps he or she used a budget you can follow. Be sure to consider the following items:

- ***Regular monthly expenses***
  - Rent, utilities, car payments, medical insurance premiums, and advocacy services.
  - The beneficiary's cash allowance, if you send one. (Be careful about giving any cash to a person who receives SSI. You don't want to reduce or eliminate the monthly benefit.)

- ***Regular annual expenses***
    - » Insurance premiums (automobile, homeowners, or renters)
    - » Vacations, including any travel costs for the beneficiary's family or staff
    - » Income taxes
- ***Occasional expenses***
    - » Computer, exercise equipment, furniture, etc. (also consider how often these items might need to be replaced)
    - » The beneficiary's "wish list" items like foreign travel or a big screen television
- ***Administrative costs***
    - » Tax preparation, accounting, bookkeeping, investment, and trustee fees
- ***Major purchases***
    - » Vehicle (including an adapted vehicle)
    - » House or condominium (also budget for repairs and capital items)

You should consider prepaying the beneficiary's funeral and burial costs. You could pay for an irrevocable funeral contract with a funeral home. You could also pay for a burial plot and a headstone if the family does not already have them. Purchasing these items while the beneficiary is living makes sense. One reason is that there might not be enough funds left when the beneficiary is gone. Another reason has to do with Medicaid. If the trust contains a so-called Medicaid payback provision, then under the Medicaid rules in most states, the state's bill for medical services will have priority over the beneficiary's funeral costs. The Medicaid agency might not allow you to use the remaining trust funds to pay for the beneficiary's funeral.

If you assign a dollar value to all the above items, then you will have a general idea of how much money you must spend each year to meet the beneficiary's needs.

The next step is to determine if your spending plan is realistic given the amount of trust funds. An accountant or financial planner can help with this task. The process involves using three variables:

- The amount of funds in the trust
- A reasonable rate of return on investments (most advisors use five to eight percent per year)
- The beneficiary's life expectancy

After you have assigned numbers to the three variables, your financial adviser can apply a formula to help you estimate how much you can spend each year without depleting the trust fund. For example, let's say you are managing a $250,000 trust for a 35-year-old beneficiary who has a life expectancy of 76 years. If the trust earns five percent a year after taxes, you should be able to spend about $14,689 per year. If you assume an eight percent rate of return after taxes, you could spend about $21,570 per year. Keep in mind that if you pay for any major expenses, such as the funeral, there will be fewer trust funds to generate income. Also, as the funds are spent, the principal is gradually drawn down, so the annual income is reduced.

What if there are not enough trust funds to meet your spending plan? In that case, you will probably have to scale back your expenditures. But this might not always be possible. Let's say the beneficiary lives in market rate housing, which the trust fund pays for. You will still have to pay for housing, even if the trust might eventually run out of money. In this situation, it might be prudent to hire an advocate to locate subsidized housing.

Be Flexible

One of the more trying aspects of managing a special needs trust is dealing with the beneficiary's requests for funds that you have not factored into your budget. The request may be perfectly legitimate —

except that it would disrupt your carefully crafted spending plan. How should you respond? The grantor probably gave you "sole discretion" to veto any request. Nevertheless, you can try to be flexible.

> You are managing a small trust for Sean, who has a once-in-a-lifetime opportunity to visit Ireland with family. The trip would cost $3,500, but you have only budgeted $1,000 for an annual vacation. You and Sean both compromise. Sean will not take a vacation the following year. He will also reduce his clothing and entertainment budget. You will pay for the vacation, even if it means slightly altering the budget, because Sean might not have the same opportunity to travel with his family again.

However, there may be times when you must refuse the beneficiary's legitimate request.

> April hates her subsidized apartment in a "boring" suburb. She wants to rent an apartment in the city near her friends. But you can't find a subsidized apartment and would have to pay market rent, which the budget does not permit. Although you sympathize with April, you must say no.

When you need to say no, telling the beneficiary your reasons can often help maintain a good relationship. Explain your decision to withhold funds and perhaps show the person a copy of your budget. In our experience, full disclosure works best. The beneficiary may not like your decision, but hopefully he or she will respect it.

Negotiation can also help. With Sean (see above), the trustee enlisted the beneficiary's help to reduce future trust expenses. In April's case, perhaps she could help you locate a subsidized apartment by filing applications with several housing authorities. You could also consider hiring a housing advocate or professional case manager to help you find subsidized housing. There are some suggestions on how to find such a person in Chapter 14, "Getting Help."

In some trustee-beneficiary relationships, conflicts about spending come up frequently. If you can establish a good working relationship with the beneficiary, your job will be much easier.

Monitor the Budget

After you develop your budget, monitor it periodically. Some trustees do this annually when they review the trust investment plan. (See Chapter 12, "Investments"). You will probably find that you need to adjust the budget from time to time in response to the beneficiary's changing circumstances.

Perhaps public benefits (such as medical insurance or subsidized housing) now cover some items you previously paid for. In that case, you can consider increasing your expenditures in other areas. Or perhaps some of the beneficiary's expenses have increased. If so, you might need to cut back in other areas. Alternatively, your financial advisor might have some ideas to generate more investment income. Whatever you decide to do, make notes of your decisions and keep them with the trust records.

The Trust Checking Account

The trust will have one or more bank accounts. Most trustees maintain a checking account to pay the regular expenses and one or more investment accounts. The specific steps to open a trust bank account are listed at the end of this section.

Be sure to use the trust's Employer Identification Number (EIN) on the accounts. (Instructions to obtain an EIN are located in Chapter 11, "Taxes.") Do not use the beneficiary's Social Security Number or your own Social Security Number. (However, the bank will probably require you to provide your Social Security Number for identification purposes.)

After you have opened the account, order checks and deposit slips with your name and the name of the trust. Be sure to keep the checkbook and checks in a safe place. Do not accept a debit card for the trust account. You should never make any cash withdrawals. The paper trail will not be adequate, and you might be accused of misusing the funds. Moreover, the trust funds could be put at risk if the card were lost or stolen.

You can also set-up electronic bill paying. Most banks offer this service. You can go online to your account and tell your bank the bills you want to pay. You don't have to bother with mailing paper checks.

New Social Security Guidelines for Certain Trust Bank Accounts Opened after January 2009

If you are opening a new self-funded trust for a beneficiary who receives SSI (or wants to qualify for that program), it is important to follow the guidelines Social Security recently enacted. These guidelines, which took effect in January 2009, apply to self-funded special needs trusts that are established by the beneficiary's parent or grandparent. The guidelines, which are located in the POMS at SI 01120.203Bf, are included in the Appendix.

Recall from Chapter 1, "The Special Needs Trust," that a person with a disability who wants to put his or her assets in a special needs trust and obtain SSI benefits cannot establish (create) the trust himself or herself. Due to a wrinkle in the law, the trust must be created by the person's parent, grandparent, or legal guardian, or by a court. The relative or guardian signs the trust document, thereby "creating" the special needs trust. The next step is for the trustee to put the beneficiary's funds in one or more trust bank accounts.

The new SSI guidelines address the establishment of the trust bank accounts. We think the guidelines are confusing, and we are not sure how they will be applied. They appear to require the parent or grandparent who has signed the trust document to use some of his or her personal funds to start the trust bank account. We suggest that you ask the parent or grandparent for a small amount of their personal funds. A check for ten dollars should be adequate. Deposit the ten dollars into the trust bank account you are opening. Then add the beneficiary's funds. As we indicated, the guidelines are not very clear. However, using a small amount of the relative's funds as the "seed" money for the trust bank account should satisfy Social Security.

How to Open a Trust Bank Account

The following are the specific steps to open a trust bank account:

- Obtain an Employer Identification Number (EIN) for the trust.

- Select the bank or investment company where you want to open the account.

- Provide the bank with the EIN, a copy of the trust, the funds to put in the account, your personal identification, such as a driver's license, and your Social Security Number. Investment companies will let you apply by mail.

- If you are opening a bank account for a new self-funded trust that was created by the beneficiary's parent or grandparent, be sure to obtain a nominal amount of money from the parent or grandparent and deposit it in the trust bank account. Do not skip this step. See the discussion earlier in this section.

- Order checks and deposit slips.

- Set-up online bill paying.

Signing your Name

Some trustees wonder how they should sign their name on documents like checks and financial accounts. We recommend that you print your name and the word "trustee" below the signature line (for example, "Sally Smith, Trustee"). Then sign your name, using your customary signature. Some trustees also write the word "trustee" after their name on the signature line.

If you sign a legal document such as a contract or a lease, you should go one step further. You should print the words, "Sally Smith as Trustee of the John Jones Trust, and not individually" below the signature line. Then sign your name, "Sally Smith, Trustee." This will make it clear to whomever you are dealing with that you are only signing the document in your capacity as the trustee. You are not a personal guarantor. If there are any problems, your personal assets will not be at risk.

Record Keeping

A good record keeping system is essential. You will need to keep accurate and complete financial records and information about the trust and the beneficiaries. You can develop a system that works for you. In general, though, your records should be organized and easy to follow. If you had to resign, someone else should be able to step in, understand how you have been managing the trust, and take over your responsibilities.

Financial Records

Most trusts generate a lot of financial paperwork. It is important to keep the trust documents well organized. This will make your job easier when it comes to preparing financial accounts (discussed later in this chapter) and income tax returns. You might also have to prepare reports for public agencies that assist the beneficiary by providing SSI, Medicaid, public housing, and/or food stamps.

Make sure there is a paper trail for every dollar that comes in or goes out of the trust. In addition to making your job easier, this is for your own protection. Even if you are doing a good job investing the trust property, you could be exposed to risk if your records are not adequate. You can never know when an unhappy beneficiary or a "concerned" third party might complain about your management. In order to meet your responsibilities, we recommend that you keep the following information organized in separate folders:

- Bank statements, cancelled checks, and check registers.

- Monthly brokerage statements and other records that show your purchase and sale of securities.

- For any individual stocks or bonds the trust owns, the date of purchase, a record of the dividends received, and the date of sale. (You might need this information for income tax purposes.)

- For any certificate of deposit (CD) the trust owns, a copy of the CD that shows the maturity date.

- Income tax returns, including back-up documentation such as 1099 forms, K-1 schedules, and brokerage statements.

- Receipts and invoices for all purchases and any notes that indicate why you thought a particular disbursement was a good idea.

- Your notes of conversations with your investment adviser (see Chapter 12, "Investments").

- A list of the trust assets with their values that you update periodically.

You should keep the trust records as long as you are in office. The beneficiaries or successor trustees may need to look at them. If the trust is large and the records are voluminous, you could consider renting storage space. You can charge the storage costs to the trust.

Personal Information about the Beneficiaries

Your trust records should also include basic personal information about all the trust beneficiaries (the beneficiary with a disability and the remainder beneficiaries). Your job will be easier because you won't have to hunt for the information you need to prepare reports, accounts, or claims. If you are taking over from a former trustee, he or she may have already prepared this information, and you can simply update it. If you are opening a new trust, you will have to start from scratch.

Often a good source of information about the primary beneficiary can be the person's parents, if they are still living. If they are not living, they may have left detailed information in a letter of intent or other written document. You might also be able to get information from the agency that serves the beneficiary.

For the *primary beneficiary,* your records should include the following kinds of information:

- *Personal information about the beneficiary*
  - » Full legal name and current address
  - » Date of birth
  - » Social Security Number
  - » Religious preference, if any
- *Information about the beneficiary's parents* (You may need this information if the beneficiary is making a claim based on a parent's work record or medical insurance benefits.)
  - » Parents' full names, addresses and dates of birth
  - » If a parent is not living, his or her date of death
- *Information about the beneficiary's income, medical insurance, and public benefits*
  - » Name and address of employer, if any
  - » For any medical insurance, the claim number and customer service telephone number
  - » Amount and kind of public benefits the person receives, such as SSI, SSDI, and housing benefits

   - » Any other income the person receives on a regular basis, such as annuity income

- *Contact information* (name, address, telephone number, and email) for people who work with or are related to the beneficiary

   - » The case manager (if any) that has been assigned by the state or hired privately to oversee the person's care
   - » The agency or service provider that supervises the person's care
   - » If the person is in residential care, the manager where the person lives
   - » The legal guardian, if there is one, otherwise the person who represents the beneficiary's interests
   - » The closest family members (parents or siblings)

- *Other information*

   - » Any final arrangements for the beneficiary, such as a pre-paid funeral contract, deed to a cemetery plot, etc.

- *Legal documents*

   - » Copy of the guardianship papers, if any

You should also keep up-to-date contact information for the *remainder beneficiaries*, including a current address and telephone number for each person. You might need to contact them about the annual accounts or to obtain their consent for certain kinds of actions.

Where to Keep the Trust Documents

The trustee is responsible for safeguarding the trust documents. These documents include the original trust instrument, any amendments to the trust, and any trustee acceptances, resignations, and appointments.

If the trust names a successor trustee, he or she should also have a copy of the trust documents.

It is important to keep these documents together in a safe place. This could be at your home or business, whatever is most convenient for you. Consider putting them in a safe deposit box or a fireproof "strong box." For extra security, some advisers recommend that you also keep a copy of the documents in a different location. Another option is to scan the documents and copy them onto one or more discs.

Accounting to the Beneficiaries

One of your duties is to provide periodic financial accounts to the beneficiaries. (The Uniform Trust Code uses the term "reports," but we prefer the traditional term "accounts.") An account is a description of the financial activities of the trust for a specific period of time, often a year. One purpose of the account is to inform the beneficiaries about the trust finances. Another purpose is to protect the trustee. In most states, you cannot be held liable for your actions if you accurately disclosed them in the account and the beneficiaries assented to them. (See Section 1009 of the Uniform Trust Code.)

Format and Contents

The format of the account will depend on the practice in your state. Some trustees include a great deal of detail (such as the date of each expenditure), while other trustees only include general categories of expenses (recreation, utilities, personal care, and so forth). Regardless of the format you use, make sure the account is clearly organized, easy to understand, and includes the following items:

- All income the trust received and a description of the source.
- All payments you made directly to the beneficiary.
- All expenses the trust paid, including trustee compensation, legal fees, taxes, bookkeeping costs, accounting expenses, and investment fees.

- Any other payments from the trust.

- The total value of the trust property at the end of the accounting period.

- The value of each item of trust property at the end of the accounting period.

Many trust accounts have three schedules. Schedule A shows the income received. Schedule B shows the expenses paid. Schedule C shows the values of the trust assets. Some trustees attach copies of the bank and investment statements that show the balances at the end of the accounting period. A sample three-schedule account is included with the Appendix.

Frequency

How often you must provide an account may be specified in the trust document. If the trust does not state the frequency, an account should be prepared annually. Some trustees provide accounts to the beneficiaries on a quarterly or even monthly basis. They recognize that the simplest way to keep a beneficiary satisfied on a long-term basis is to provide him or her with frequent detailed accounts of the trust activities.

If you take over a trust from a prior trustee, it is important to have your predecessor prepare a final account and have the beneficiaries approve it. In some states, you could be liable for the prior trustee's actions if his or her account has not been approved.

If you resign as the trustee or are ready to close the trust, you must provide a final account. The trustee's final account is explained in Chapter 13, "Closing the Trust."

Who is Entitled to Receive the Accounts

The trust document might specify who is entitled to receive the accounts. The Uniform Trust Code requires you to send the accounts to the beneficiary with a disability. [sec. 813(c)] Even if the beneficiary cannot understand the information in the account, he or she is still entitled to receive a copy of the document. If the beneficiary has a legal representative, we suggest that you send your account to that person. The legal representative could be the beneficiary's legal guardian, conservator, or someone the beneficiary has nominated to act for him or her under a power of attorney.

The remainder beneficiaries should also be given copies of the accounts if they request them. The remainder beneficiaries are the individuals who will receive any funds that are left in the trust when the lifetime beneficiary dies and the trust ends.

Obtain the Beneficiaries' Written Agreement

In addition to satisfying the beneficiary and his or her legal representative, a proper account may provide some protection to you as well. Most trust documents prohibit the beneficiaries from challenging the trustee on any particular matter (such as a specific expense or an investment loss) after a certain period of time has passed. A common provision gives the beneficiary (or his or her legal representative) a 90-day period to object to an account. If the beneficiary has not responded after 90 days, he or she has lost the right to object. Your state might have its own rules. Under the Uniform Trust Code, if a beneficiary has assented in writing to the account, he or she may not object later [section 1009].

We recommend that whenever you send an account to a beneficiary, you also send an Assent form and ask the person to sign it. (A sample Assent form is located in the Appendix.) It is always preferable to have the beneficiaries approve your accounts rather than not respond to them. However, under the Uniform Trust Code, even if the beneficiary did not assent in writing, he or she may not challenge the account if more than a year has elapsed since the account was provided [section 1005].

There are some instances where the beneficiary's failure to respond will not protect you. You could probably be held liable if the account you gave the beneficiary was not proper, or if you did not give the account to someone who was entitled to receive it. In that case, the account could be reopened at any time and your actions could be examined.

Of course, even the beneficiaries' written agreement to an account will not protect a trustee who engages in fraud or misappropriates the trust property.

Chapter 11
Taxes

Tax reporting is one of the trustee's primary responsibilities. You must make sure that all trust income is properly reported and the taxes are paid on time. If you don't, the trust might have to pay interest and penalties.

The following discussion of taxes and the special needs trust is intended to help you navigate this complicated area. However, these materials are intended for general guidance only. If you need tax advice about any specific situation, be sure to consult a qualified tax professional who is knowledgeable about public benefits and special needs trusts.

Notifying the Internal Revenue Service about the Trust

If you are opening a new trust, you should notify the Internal Revenue Service that the trust has been created. You do this by applying for an Employer Identification Number (EIN). Also, the first time you file any trust income tax returns, you must notify the IRS that you are the trustee. To do so, use Form 56 (described below). Your state might also have its own notification requirements. Your tax advisor can tell you about them.

The Employer Identification Number

A special needs trust should have its own Employer Identification Number. An EIN is used by the IRS to identify businesses and trusts. After you obtain the EIN, be sure to use it on all the trust accounts. Do not use the beneficiary's Social Security Number or your own Social Security Number.

You can obtain an EIN by filing Form SS-4 ("Application for Employer Identification Number"). The IRS will also issue an EIN over the telephone (1-800-829-4933) or online at http://www.irs.gov. If you apply by telephone, you (the trustee) must personally speak with the IRS representative and provide the following information:

- Name of the trust
- Name of the grantor (see below)
- Grantor's Social Security Number (see below)
- Name of the trustee
- Trustee's address
- Trustee's Social Security Number
- Trustee's date of birth

An SS-4 form and instructions are located in the Appendix.

Identifying the "grantor" on the SS-4 form can be tricky because it is not necessarily the person who is called the grantor in the trust document. For IRS purposes, the grantor is the person whose money was initially placed in the trust. This could be the beneficiary or someone else.

- If the beneficiary put his or her own funds in the trust, he or she is the "grantor" for tax purposes. This is true even though someone else may be called the "grantor" in the trust document. Due to a wrinkle in the law, some kinds of special needs trusts can only be created by the beneficiary's parent, grandparent, legal guardian, or a court. That person (or the court) is usually called the "grantor" on the trust document. Nevertheless, the beneficiary's Social Security Number should be provided to the IRS on the SS-4 form — not the Social Security Number of the parent, grandparent, or guardian.

- If a third party (such as a parent of the beneficiary) put his or her own funds in the trust, then the third party is the grantor, and his or her Social Security Number should be used on the SS-4 form.

Form 56

If you are signing the income tax return for the first time as the trustee, you must file IRS Form 56 ("Notice Concerning Fiduciary Relationship"). You should also complete this form if you are taking over the trust as the successor trustee. Otherwise, the IRS might not recognize you as the legal representative of the trust. You do not need to apply for a new Employer Identification Number, because it remains the same for the life of the trust. Form 56 is located in the Appendix.

Tax Treatment of the Initial Trust Funds

In most cases, the trust funds are not subject to any federal or state income tax when they are initially placed in the trust. This is true whether the trust is a self-funded trust or a third party trust.[19]

With a self-funded trust, the beneficiary may have placed the proceeds from a personal injury lawsuit in the trust. The proceeds would be tax-free regardless of whether the award was paid as a lump sum or in installments through an annuity. (However, any pre- or post-judgment interest would be taxable.)

With a third party trust, a deceased person may have left money directly to the trust. In most cases, the trust's receipt of the inheritance would not generate a tax. However, depending on the size of the estate that paid the inheritance, an estate tax might be owed. In that case, any estate tax would have been paid by the estate before the funds were distributed to the trust. A few states impose inheritance taxes. Such taxes are paid by the recipients of estate property. In these states, the trust might owe an inheritance tax. Your tax advisor can tell you if that is the case for the trust you are managing.

---

[19] A self-funded trust (also called a first party trust) contains assets that belonged to the beneficiary before they were put in the trust. A third party trust contains assets that belonged to someone other than the beneficiary, such as a parent or grandparent, before they were put in the trust. See Chapter 1, "The Special Needs Trust."

Income Taxes and the Special Needs Trust

When the trust funds are invested, they may generate earnings such as interest, dividends, and capital gains. In general, the trust must pay income taxes on these kinds of earnings. The only exceptions are municipal bonds, which do not generate taxable income. In some cases, the income tax on interest may be deferred. For example, income on series EE Savings Bonds is not taxable until the bonds are redeemed.

The trust might owe a capital gains tax if it sells an investment for a price that is higher than the purchase price. These capital gains may be short-term or long-term, depending on how long the asset was owned. Some states and municipalities impose their own income taxes. You should consult with a tax advisor to find out if this is the case in your state.

If the trust has any taxable income, or if it has income over $600, you must file a federal income tax return. You must also determine whether the taxes will be paid by the trust itself or by the beneficiary. In general, this will depend on whether the trust is a self-funded trust or a third party trust.

Self-funded Trust

In most cases, if the trust was self-funded, the beneficiary — not the trust — will pay any income taxes. The IRS will "look through" the trust and treat the beneficiary as the taxpayer. Under the grantor trust rules, any earnings and deductions must be "passed through" to the beneficiary, who will report them on his or her personal income tax return. This is true even if the income is accumulated in the trust and not distributed.

> Donna is the beneficiary of a self-funded special needs trust that contains her personal injury settlement. In one year, the trust earns $8,000, which it accumulates and does not spend. The trust passes through $8,000 of income to Donna. Donna will report the income on her personal income tax return. The trust will not pay any income tax.

A grantor trust usually presents a favorable income tax situation. The trust itself does not have to pay any income tax because it can pass its income through to the beneficiary. The beneficiary might not have to pay any income tax either. Most single individuals under age 65 do not need to pay any tax if their income is less than $9,350 (in 2010). Many beneficiaries do not have that level of income ($9,350). SSI is not taxed, and SSDI is not taxed if a single person's total income — including one-half of SSDI benefits — is less than $25,000.

In terms of income tax reporting, the trust files IRS Form 1041. However, this can be a brief "information" return. It shows the income received and any allowable deductions, such as medical expenses, taxes, and mortgage interest. Form 1041 contains the beneficiary's Social Security Number and states that all income and deductions are being passed through to the beneficiary. The trustee will send the beneficiary a schedule K-1 that shows the income and deductions. The beneficiary puts the information from the K-1 form on his or her personal income tax return (Form 1040).

As for state income taxes, each state has its own rules for reporting and paying taxes. Your tax professional can assist you with the filing requirements and forms.

Third Party Trust

A third party trust is a separate taxable entity that must pay income tax on its earnings. (A third party trust is one that contains property that belonged to someone other than the beneficiary before it was put in the trust.) A third party trust can present a potentially disadvantageous income tax situation. The income tax rates for trusts range from 15 percent to 35 percent, and the tax brackets rise steeply as compared to personal income tax rates. For example, in 2009, an individual did not reach the 35% maximum tax rate until he or she had $372,950 of taxable income. However, in 2009, a trust reached the 35% maximum tax rate with only $11,150 of taxable income.

> Marcia is the beneficiary of a third party trust. In one year, the trust earns $15,000 in interest and dividends, which it

accumulates and does not spend. The trust does not pay any administrative costs. The trust is not a qualified disability trust (discussed below), so it can only take a $100 exemption (also discussed below). The trust will pay taxes of $4,292 (in 2009).

Fortunately, it may be possible to avoid paying large amounts of tax on the trust earnings, because the law only requires a trust to pay taxes on its net income. (The technical term is distributable net income, or DNI.) For a special needs trust, there are three principal ways a trust can reduce its total income to arrive at net income.

- The trust can deduct its reasonable administrative expenses, including:

    - » Taxes, like state and local income taxes, real estate taxes, and personal property taxes.

    - » Trustee fees and any direct expenses the trustee incurs, such as travel expenses and out of pocket costs.

    - » Professional fees, including attorney, accountant, tax preparer, and bookkeeper costs.

- The trust can claim a general exemption of either $100 or $3,650 (in 2009). The larger amount applies if the trust can be considered a *qualified disability trust* under section 642 of the Internal Revenue Code (discussed later in this section).

- The trust can deduct any income it distributes directly to the beneficiary or spends on his or her behalf. The trustee reports all such amounts on schedule K-1, which it sends to the IRS and the beneficiary. The beneficiary reports all K-1 income on his or her personal income tax return and pays tax at his or her personal rate, which is almost always lower than the trust rate.

For Marcia (see above), suppose the trust earned $15,000, paid $3,000 in administrative costs, and spent $15,000 for Marcia's rent and car payments. The trust will not pay any income tax. It can deduct all its administrative costs, take the $100 exemption, and deduct the remaining net income it spent on Marcia's behalf. Marcia will report $12,000 of income on her personal income tax return ($15,000 of trust income less $3,000 of administrative costs = $12,000). Assuming that she is single, under age 65, and is not claimed as a dependent on another person's income tax return, Marcia would pay federal income tax of $308. (The amount of state tax, if any, would depend on the state where Marcia lives.)

Qualified Disability Trust

If the trust is a qualified disability trust for income tax purposes, the exemption amount is the same amount as the beneficiary's personal exemption. (The personal exemption, which is $3,650 in 2009, increases each year.) To be considered a qualified disability trust, the trust must meet the following requirements:

- The trust must have been established for a beneficiary with a disability under age 65.

- The beneficiary with a disability must be the sole beneficiary (although the remainder beneficiaries can be individuals without disabilities or organizations such as charities).

- The trust cannot be considered a "grantor" trust for tax purposes. This means that the person who funded the trust cannot be the trustee or control how the trust funds will be used. Also, the grantor must give up any right to get the trust property back, even if the beneficiary dies before him or her.

The following example shows how a qualified disability trust can use the general exemption to reduce its taxable income.

> Bob is the beneficiary of a qualified disability trust that earned $10,000 in income (interest and dividends) in 2009. That year, the trustee paid $3,000 in administrative costs (for trustee fees and tax preparation) but did not distribute any other trust funds. The trust can use Bob's personal exemption ($3,650). Thus, the trust has taxable income of $3,450 ($10,000 - $3,000 - $3,650 = $3,450). The tax will amount to $608.

In the above example, assume that Bob's special needs trust does not meet the requirements to be a qualified disability trust. It can only take a $100 exemption.

> For Bob (see above), the special needs trust does not meet the requirements to be a qualified disability trust. In 2009, the trust earned $10,000. The trustee paid $3,000 in administrative costs but did not distribute any other trust funds. The trust can only take a $100 exemption. The trust will pay tax on income of $6,900 ($10,000 - $3,000 - $100 = $6,900). The tax will amount to $1,542.

State Income Taxes

As far as state income taxes are concerned, each state has its own rules. For example, Massachusetts does not permit a third party trust to deduct the income it distributes. Your tax advisor can tell you about the rules in your state.

Reducing Income Taxes

If you are concerned about the amount of income taxes the trust is paying, you could consider strategies to reduce them. One way to reduce income taxes is to invest the trust funds in assets that produce non-taxable income. Some examples are:

- ***Growth-oriented stocks.*** These companies reinvest their earnings in capital projects (such as buildings or new equipment) instead of paying them as dividends.

- ***Tax-free investments*** such as municipal bonds. However, these kinds of investments usually pay lower interest than comparable taxable investments.

- ***Deferred-income assets*** such as Series EE Savings Bonds or a tax-deferred annuity. You do not pay tax on the interest from a Savings Bond until you redeem the bond or it matures. With a tax-deferred annuity, taxes on income are postponed until you draw payments from the annuity.

Another way to reduce the trust's income taxes is to distribute the trust's income to the beneficiary or use it to pay the beneficiary's bills. As we explained earlier in this chapter, a third party trust does not have to pay income tax on any money it distributes. The distributions can be passed through to the beneficiary, reported as income on his or her personal income tax return, and taxed at the beneficiary's income tax rate. However, before proceeding, there are a couple of things to consider:

- Distributing the trust's income must be consistent with your overall plan for managing the trust. For example, if the beneficiary does not need very much from the trust and you are saving the assets for future years, it would not make sense to distribute the funds to the beneficiary simply to reduce income taxes.

- You must also take into account the impact that any distributions would have on the beneficiary's government benefits. As we explain throughout this book, if the beneficiary receives SSI, you should avoid giving him or her any cash or paying for food and housing items. If the beneficiary lives in public housing, you must be careful about giving him or her money from the trust or paying bills on a regular basis. Most regular payments will be viewed by the public housing authority as "income" that will increase the person's monthly rent. Chapter 7, "Housing," explains how the housing authorities treat payments of income from a trust.

Income Taxes and SSI

We explained earlier in this chapter that when a trust earns income like interest and dividends, someone must report the income and pay the tax. Sometimes the trust reports the income on the trust tax return (Form 1041). In other cases, the trustee elects to have the income reflected on the beneficiary's personal income tax return. This approach can often result in substantial tax savings. The individual tax rates are usually lower than the trust tax rates. In addition, an individual can often claim a larger exemption than a trust ($3,650 for an individual in 2009, versus $100 for most trusts). The tax laws allow the trust income to be reported on the beneficiary's personal return, even though the beneficiary may not have actually received the income. The trustee usually writes a check to pay for any taxes the beneficiary owes.

Reporting the trust income on the beneficiary's income tax return can sometimes cause a problem if the beneficiary receives SSI. The beneficiary may have reported little or no income to Social Security — yet the tax filings show thousands of dollars of income received. Social Security may suspect that the beneficiary has received income he or she did not report. The agency may send a letter of inquiry or even summon the beneficiary to come to a meeting.

If this occurs with the trust you are managing, you should provide a copy of the 1041 return and the schedules to the beneficiary (or the person who is helping him or her with the SSI benefits). You might also write a letter to Social Security describing what took place. The letter should explain that the assets that earned the interest and dividends belong to the trust — not the beneficiary. The letter would also state that you did not give any of the trust's income directly to the beneficiary. Although the beneficiary may have received income "on paper" for tax purposes, he or she did not receive any income (cash, food, or housing) for SSI program purposes.

Retirement Accounts

The special needs trust may be named as the beneficiary of a retirement account, such as an IRA, 401(k) or 403(b) account, or a Roth IRA. These accounts normally receive favorable income tax treatment as deferred income. However, they are subject to complicated rules for taking withdrawals from the account, both for the original owner and any person who inherits the account after the original owner has died. In most cases, the funds that are withdrawn from a retirement account are taxable.

If you learn that the special needs trust is the beneficiary of a retirement account, you will need to contact the person administering the estate of the original owner, the administrator of the funds (which may be a bank or investment firm), and in the case of a 401(k) or 403(b) account, the employer of the original owner. Depending on how the rules for withdrawals apply to your particular situation, you may be able to stretch out the payments from the account and thus reduce income taxes. If the special needs trust is not required to take all the account funds at one time but can instead take out the funds in annual or other periodic installments, the tax impact will be less. You will have until December 31 of the year following the original owner's death to decide how the special needs trust will withdraw the funds. It is essential to get competent advice about how to deal with the retirement account from your financial adviser, attorney, or accountant.

In order to make the best choice about withdrawing the funds from the retirement account, you should obtain the following information:

- ***A copy of the trust.*** The advisor will need to review the trust document to determine if it qualifies for favorable income tax treatment. To qualify, the trust must meet four basic requirements:

    - » The trust must be irrevocable by its terms, or have become irrevocable on the death of the original account owner.
    - » The trust must be valid under state law.
    - » The trust must name beneficiaries who can be identified.
    - » The administrator must have been given a copy of the trust while the original account owner was living.

- ***The age of the original account owner when he or she died.*** The rules for distributions are different depending on whether the owner was age 70 ½ or older, or under age 70 ½ as of the owner's date of death.

- ***The relationship between the trust beneficiary and the original owner.*** If the beneficiary is the owner's spouse, there are more generous rules for taking withdrawals from the retirement account.

- ***The ages of the beneficiary with a disability and all remainder beneficiaries of the special needs trust.*** A remainder beneficiary is the one who will receive the trust benefits after the beneficiary with a disability has died. When the beneficiary of a retirement account is a trust, the payout schedule is based on the age of the oldest beneficiary of the trust, even if that person is a remainder beneficiary.

- ***For a Roth IRA, the date the account was opened.*** In most cases, any funds withdrawn from a Roth IRA are not taxable. But if the account has been open less than five years, the withdrawals may be subject to income tax. This is also the case after the original account owner has died.

- ***For a 401(k) or 403(b) account, a copy of the plan's rules for distributions.*** Some account administrators refuse to hold an account open in order to make distributions over a period of years. Instead, they require the beneficiary to take a single lump sum payment or roll the account into an IRA, if that is permitted.

This information should help you and your adviser withdraw the retirement funds in a way that will minimize the income taxes.

In addition to income taxes, you must also consider whether the withdrawals will affect any or all of the public benefits the beneficiary receives. Your attorney can help you with this.

Estate Taxes

In some cases when the beneficiary of a self-funded trust dies, estate taxes may be owed on the beneficiary's estate. Estate taxes are a very complicated topic. Most special needs trusts are not affected because of the large amounts of money needed before an estate tax is owed. (See "federal estate tax limits" below. Most likely only estates worth more than $3.5 million will be taxed in 2010). Estate taxes are not usually a factor until the beneficiary has died and the trust is being closed. In Chapter 13, "Closing the Trust," we will walk you through the steps to conclude the trust business and distribute the remaining assets. In that chapter, we advise you to work closely with an attorney to make sure that any taxes — including estate taxes — are paid before you distribute the remaining funds.

Nevertheless, there is one situation where you might want to anticipate the potential payment of estate taxes and plan for them while the beneficiary is still living. That is when the trust will be receiving income payments from an annuity after the beneficiary has died. At the end of this chapter, we explain how life insurance can be used to pay estate taxes that may be due on an annuity when the beneficiary of a self-funded trust dies.

Federal Estate Tax Limits

As this book is being written (in 2010), there is a great deal of uncertainty about the future of the federal estate tax. Under the current law, the estates of persons who die in 2010 will not be taxed. In 2011, estates worth more than $1 million will be taxed. Many analysts expect Congress to change the law to provide that estates worth more than $3.5 million will be taxed. However, there is no consensus about what Congress may do.

State Estate Taxes

Some states impose their own estate taxes with limits that are lower than the federal amounts. In Massachusetts, for example, any amounts over $1 million are subject to an estate tax.

Property that is Included in the Estate Tax

The property that would be subject to the estate tax includes both the beneficiary's own property as well as any property that is left in the trust when the beneficiary dies. This amount can be reduced by expenses like the beneficiary's funeral expenses, his or her outstanding debts, any costs incurred to settle the beneficiary's estate or to close the trust, and the beneficiary's unpaid medical expenses, including the full amount of Medicaid that must be paid back to the state.

Estate Taxes and Annuities

Some self-funded trusts own an annuity. An annuity pays income at fixed intervals for a specific length of time, such as a period of years or a person's lifetime. If the payments will continue after the beneficiary's death, an estate tax could be owed when the beneficiary dies.

To illustrate, let's say the trust owns an annuity that will pay income to the trust for thirty years. The beneficiary dies in the fifth year. The value of the next twenty-five years of payments is an asset of the beneficiary's taxable estate. To arrive at the value of the future payments, you can't just add them up. You will need an accountant to employ a complicated formula that includes factors like an assumed rate of interest and discounts.

The estate tax is due nine months after the beneficiary's death. It is important to pay the estate tax promptly, because interest and substantial penalties are charged on any unpaid amounts. For an additional charge, some annuities provide that if the beneficiary dies before all the payments have been made, part of the remaining value of the annuity will be paid in a lump sum. You can use the lump sum to pay the estate tax. But if the annuity does not have this feature, you will have to find another way to pay the tax. If the estate does not have sufficient assets, you will have to wait for the future annuity payments to arrive. In the meantime, interest will accrue on the unpaid tax. This can cause a significant economic problem for the trust, because many of the future annuity payments could be consumed by the estate tax and interest.

A way to solve this problem is to purchase an insurance policy on the beneficiary's life. The proceeds from the policy can be used to pay the estate tax due upon the beneficiary's death. You will need to know how much life insurance to buy. The insurance agent who sold the annuity (or the company for which he or she works) can calculate the annuity's value for any particular year. This will tell you how much life insurance would be needed if the beneficiary died in that year. As time passes and some of the annuity payments are made, the value of the annuity will decrease. Then the amount of life insurance can be reduced.

CHAPTER 12

Investments

Investing the trust funds can be one of the trustee's most important — and challenging — responsibilities. You are expected to produce a reasonable rate of return for the beneficiary, yet you cannot take undue risks. There may be restrictions under state law or in the trust document that limit how you can invest the funds. Fortunately, there are qualified financial advisers who can help you understand your responsibilities or even take over investing the funds for you. This chapter explains how to meet your basic responsibilities in this important area.

Making the Trust Productive

One of your responsibilities as the trustee is to make the trust "productive." Essentially this means that the trust assets must generate a reasonable amount of earnings for the beneficiary. You can't just let the money sit in a non-interest bearing checking account. Does this mean you have to invest in the stock market? Probably, because the laws in most states require you to "diversify" the trust investments in a mix of stocks, bonds, and cash, unless there is a specific reason not to do so.

Making the trust productive can be challenging. The appropriate strategy will depend on several factors, including the beneficiary's age, needs, and health status. For example, if the beneficiary is young and healthy, you might emphasize long term growth by having more stocks than bonds. On the other hand, if the beneficiary is older, you might invest more conservatively by having more bonds than stocks. In most cases, funds in a special needs trust should be invested conservatively. The trust funds will have to last the beneficiary's lifetime. Still, you can't let the trust fund erode by investing too conservatively — and this usually requires investing in stocks and bonds. In short, there are different routes you can take. Choosing the best route is not always simple.

Risks that you might take with your own money may not be appropriate for the trust's money. Investing for unrealistically high returns could lead to disastrous consequences. Acting on "hot tips" or "gut feelings" is not the way to go. Instead, you must act in a prudent, reasonable manner. This may include looking at companies whose names and products are unfamiliar, but whose results, while not stellar, are consistently positive. It might also mean investing more money in the bond market, which is generally not in the news, and less money in the stock market, which is always in the news. When it comes to investing for a special needs trust, safe and secure is best.

Limits on Investments

Before you commit to a specific investment strategy, you should find out if the terms of the trust or the laws in your state limit your ability to invest the trust funds in any particular manner. Your attorney or financial adviser can assist you with this. The following are some common restrictions that you might encounter.

The Uniform Prudent Investor Act

Every state except Louisiana has passed some version of the Uniform Prudent Investor Act, which governs investments by trustees. A list of citations for each state is included in the Appendix. Your attorney can help you locate the statute in your state and review its provisions. Most state laws require you to do things like diversify the investments, avoid conflicts of interest, and minimize investment costs.

The Trust Document

Some trust documents prohibit the trustee from purchasing certain kinds of investments, such as stocks. We have seen special needs trusts that require the trustee to buy ultra-safe items like government-backed securities (Treasury bills, municipal bonds, etc.). If the trust you are managing contains this kind of restriction, you must adhere to it. This is required by Section 1 of the Uniform Prudent Investor Act.

Conflicts of Interest

You should never invest the trust funds in any way that benefits yourself, your friends, or your relatives. That means no private loans for a cousin's fledgling business or a niece's tuition costs. Besides being risky, these kinds of transactions violate your fiduciary duty to make investment decisions solely for the benefit of the beneficiary. No one should receive a benefit from the trust simply because they are your friend or relative.

Social Investing

A trustee should not practice so-called social investing. In this form of investing, you make investment decisions based on your personal social or political values. Most social investors avoid buying stock in companies that produce things like weapons, tobacco, and furs, and favor ones that are family- or environmentally-friendly. While social investing might be laudable in your personal life, it is not proper for a trustee. You are not supposed to subordinate the interests of the beneficiary to a particular social cause or political purpose.

A Framework for Investments

Before you purchase stocks, bonds, and mutual funds, you should develop a framework for investments. We list some specific steps you can take. We recommend that you hire a financial adviser to assist you. If you are going to hire an investment firm to take over the investments, as we discuss in the next section, your account manager at the investment firm can help you with these tasks.

- *Perform an initial review.* If you are taking over from another trustee, you must review the trust assets within a reasonable period of time after you become the trustee. This is required by Section 4 of the Uniform Prudent Investor Act. Your adviser can tell you whether the assets are producing a reasonable rate of return, are safe, and are suited for the particular trust you are managing.

- *Set goals.* Most financial advisers recommend that you set measurable goals you want to achieve. The goal could be tied to a tangible purpose, like making sure the beneficiary can draw $1,000 per month from the trust fund for the next five years, and then $1,500 per month for the following seven years Alternatively, the goal could be tied to a specific benchmark, like meeting or exceeding the Standard and Poor Index in three out of the next five years. This might be appropriate for a beneficiary who has very few financial needs and does not draw much, if anything, from the trust.

- *Assess your level of risk.* Your adviser can help you judge the level of risk you are willing to assume to meet your goals. Some assets like stocks are often riskier than others, such as bonds and money market funds. Yet stocks have usually generated greater returns than bonds. Of course, as recent history has shown, if you invest in the stock market, you can risk losing a substantial amount of your investment. If you must take an inordinate risk to meet your goals, you will have to scale back your goals.

- ***Devise an investment strategy.*** Your investment adviser can help you allocate the investments in a specific ratio of stocks, bonds, and cash. For example, an allocation for a special needs trust might be 50% stocks, 40% bonds, and 10% cash. However, the specific allocation will be based on your investment goals and the level of risk you are willing to accept.

Investing the Trust Funds

Most trust documents authorize the trustee to pay for professional assistance with investments. Some even encourage you to do so. Unless you are an experienced (and successful) investor, we recommend that you hire someone. The professional's fees are tax deductible. Moreover, hiring someone might protect you if the trust loses money.

There are many choices for investment help. These range from one-person firms to large investment firms, banks, and trust companies. The best choice is a person (or firm) that has a good reputation and is recommended by someone whose judgment you trust. However, if the trust has $100,000 or less, your choices may be limited. Even a one-person firm may not accept such a small account. You can still obtain help with investments, but you will have to do most of the work yourself with limited assistance from a professional.

Working with an Account Manager

When you sign up with an investment firm, you will be assigned to an account manager. (If you hire your financial adviser to take over the investments, he or she will take on the role of an account manager. Later in this chapter we will explain the financial adviser's role.) Your account manager will help you develop investment goals and make an initial allocation of the investments among stocks, bonds, and cash. Then the manager will select the investments, monitor them, and periodically decide to keep or sell them. The manager will meet with you from time to time — perhaps two or three times a year, more often if necessary. The firm will also send you monthly statements of the account activity.

An initial decision you must make is how much authority you will delegate to the account manager. Will you give the manager free rein to decide on the investments, or do you want to be consulted about each transaction? This will depend on your preferences, the terms of the trust, and the laws in your state.

- *Your preferences.* Some trustees don't want to give the account manager broad latitude to make investment choices. They prefer to be consulted about each transaction. If this is your preference, be sure to let the manager know this.

- *The laws in your state.* Section 9 of the Uniform Prudent Investor Act permits a trustee to delegate decisions about investments to an outside manager. However, if your state has not adopted this particular section of the Act and the terms of the trust you are managing do not permit you to delegate (see below), you must retain final authority over all purchases and sales of investments by the trust.

- *The terms of the trust.* Some trust documents limit your ability to delegate to an outside manager. This is fairly rare because most trusts written in the last twenty years adopt the broad language of the Uniform Prudent Investor Act that allows trustees to delegate investment decisions to an investment professional. Your attorney can tell you if this is the case with the trust you are managing. The legal department of the investment company you will be working with can also review the trust document and tell you if there are any limitations.

Assuming there are no restrictions on your ability to delegate, and you have turned over all investment decisions to your account manager, your responsibilities have not ended. You still have to monitor the manager's activities. You should review the monthly account statements to make sure the funds are accounted for. Keep notes of all telephone conversations and save any email correspondence. Last, every year or so, you should review the entire account to see if you have met your goals.

Professional managers are paid based on the amount of assets under management. The fees usually range from .5 to 2 percent of the market value of the portfolio per year. Often the fees are negotiable, depending on the size of the trust and the level of activity. In general, the larger the trust, the smaller the percentage that will be charged. The fees might be in the higher range if the account requires active management because the beneficiary needs a substantial number of distributions. The fees are usually charged quarterly, based on the value of the portfolio at the end of the prior quarter.

Be sure there is a written agreement that describes the fees to be charged, the services the manager will provide, and how much authority you will delegate to the manager. A requirement of the Uniform Prudent Investor Act is that a trustee must exercise care, skill, and caution in establishing the terms of delegation [sec. 4]. In order to meet your responsibilities, you should not necessarily accept the standard agreements offered by most management firms. Read the fine print. Provisions that might be acceptable for your personal account might not be permissible for a trust. If possible, avoid an agreement that allows the manager to purchase his or her own products without a fee adjustment ("double dipping"), or one that absolves the manager of liability for mismanagement.

Last, you have to be selective about who you hire. If the trust incurs a loss because the person is grossly unqualified — or worse, dishonest — you might have to bear the financial consequences. We provide some suggestions about how to locate a qualified person in Chapter 14, "Getting Help."

Investing the Trust Funds Yourself

If the trust is too small to attract an investment firm, you can hire a financial adviser at an hourly rate. The person can help you with the tasks we described earlier in this chapter (see a Framework for Investments). These tasks include performing an initial review, setting goals, and allocating the trust funds in a particular ratio of stocks, bonds, and cash. The person can also make specific recommendations as to which mutual funds you should purchase.

Even with a small trust, it is important to keep the investment costs reasonable. You should evaluate the fees charged by mutual funds. If you plan to purchase individual stocks or bonds, discount brokers such as Ameritrade and Etrade offer low commissions.

Good record keeping is also important. Be sure to keep track of maturing certificates of deposit, bonds, etc. A good practice is to develop a simple accounting system to monitor the investments. That way, you can know at any time how much the trust is worth. Some trustees like the Quicken or Excel financial software programs for this purpose.

Educating Yourself

It is important to have a basic understanding of investments. This is true even if you have delegated the investment tasks to a professional. To be an effective trustee, you must understand the recommendations your adviser is giving and make an educated decision before you accept or reject them. Understanding investments is even more important if you have minimal (or no) help from a financial professional. The Appendix to this chapter ("Investment Basics") can get you started. For general reading on investing, we like *The Only Investment Guide You'll Ever Need* by Andrew Tobias (listed in Chapter 16, "Resources").

Limiting Your Liability

Some trustees worry that if the trust loses money, they might forfeit their position or even be held personally liable. In our experience, trustees are rarely, if ever, held personally responsible for investment losses. There is a good deal of protection for trustees under the Uniform Prudent Investment Act, as long as you adhere to its provisions. You will be protected as long as you exercise reasonable "care, skill, and caution" in managing the assets (or use reasonable care, skill, and caution in choosing someone to manage them for you and then monitor the person). What if one or more of your investments loses money in any particular year? Fortunately, your investment decisions will be judged in the context of the trust portfolio as a whole, instead of individually. [Uniform Prudent Investor Act, sec. 4] The following are some steps you can take to protect yourself:

- Read the trust document and familiarize yourself with any provisions regarding investments.

- Learn about the laws in your state that govern investments by trustees, and avoid any prohibited transactions.

- Do not under any circumstances borrow money from the trust or lend it to your family or friends.

- Diversify the investments in a mix of stocks, bonds, and cash, unless there are special reasons why you should not do so.

- If you hire an account manager to invest the trust funds, use care, skill, and caution in selecting the person, and regularly monitor the person's activities.

- Keep investment costs reasonable. Make sure there is a written fee agreement that spells out the costs. Review the adviser's bills to make sure the charges are accurate and appropriate. If the person is over-charging you, terminate the relationship and hire someone else.

Appendix to Chapter 12

Investment Basics

As the trustee, you realize you have to "invest" the trust's money. But what exactly does that mean? You know that some money will be put in stocks, but you aren't really sure what a stock is. You hear that bonds might be "safer" than stocks, but you don't understand how a bond works. You are advised that the trust's investments should be diversified, but you aren't really sure what that means either. You have an investment adviser, but you never completely grasp what he or she is saying.

This section covers five basic areas: stocks, bonds, cash, mutual funds, and diversification. It answers questions like, what are stocks and bonds? How do they work and how are they measured? What role does cash play? What is diversification and why is it important?

Being able to answer these questions will put you in a better position to judge how the trust is performing. It will also give you a more realistic sense of what is (and is not) possible. Ultimately, as trustee, you are the person who will decide what course the trust takes. You will also be the first person the beneficiary (or his or her family) calls with questions about the trust's investments. (This is especially true when things don't go as planned.) Understanding a few basic investment concepts can help to make your job a little less daunting. It can also help you become a better trustee.

This section is not a comprehensive analysis of how money is invested. The study of investments is a vast and complex field. We are not in a position to identify particular investments or strategies that should or should not be followed. Instead, our goal is limited to offering a brief overview of some key concepts.

In most cases, one of your first steps should be to consult with an experienced financial adviser. This is especially true if you are not experienced with investments. A good financial adviser can offer direction and guidance. Other individuals, such as family members, friends and acquaintances, might offer their advice. However, this is one area where trying to save a little money by relying on such advice could end up costing a great deal more. Working with an experienced financial adviser is usually the best approach. More information on investment advisers can be found in Chapter 14, "Getting Help."

Investing in Difficult Economic Times

At the time that this chapter is being written, the American economy is going through a severe crisis. The value of many companies has declined quickly and dramatically. Credit (the ability to obtain a loan) has tightened substantially for both individuals and businesses. Enormous amounts of money have been lost, and the federal government has taken unprecedented actions in response.

The financial sector has been particularly hard hit. Some of the largest businesses in the nation have turned to the government for help. Others have been forced into mergers or simply closed their doors. These problems have now spread across the globe. Many analysts believe that a very difficult period lies ahead.

Historically, the American economy has gone through repeated expansions and recessions. Although each recession brings financial hardship and loss, the economy does eventually rebound. Most recessions last for months not years. Successful companies do emerge, money is made, and the economy resumes growing. Over the long term, investing in stocks and bonds has been relatively profitable when compared to keeping everything in cash. History suggests that this pattern will not change. For that reason, the investment concepts discussed in this chapter will be relevant in any economic climate.

Stocks

A stock is an ownership interest in a company. (Stocks are also referred to as equities.) A company will issue stock as a way to raise money. For example, the owner of ABC Corporation may have an idea for a great new product. However, buying the machine to make that product costs more than the owner has in the bank. Convinced that his idea is a sure winner, the owner may agree to sell part of ABC Corporation to other people. With the money raised from these other investors (the new stockholders), the owner is able to purchase the machine that he needs to get going.

A profitable company that has issued stock often pays a dividend four times a year. Paying a dividend is a way for the company to distribute some of its profit to its stockholders. Some companies do not pay any dividend; instead, these companies reinvest all of their profits for future growth. Other companies may not pay a dividend because there is no profit left to distribute.

A dividend might be as little as a few cents per share. However, if a stockholder has thousands of shares in a company, the dividend could add up to a substantial amount. When someone speaks of investing for income, they usually mean looking at the size and consistency of the company's dividend. Some investors simply want a steady stream of income that they can receive on a reliable basis.

Another way that an investor can earn money is by selling his stock at a gain. As a company's prospects improve, the price that other investors are willing to pay for the company's stock increases. Investing for growth means looking for companies whose stock price might rise substantially. For these investors, the company's dividend is a secondary concern. However, while "aggressive" investing might sound great, it also means taking on more risk.

Until shares are actually sold, any gain is only "on paper." This means that the gain could be reduced or disappear altogether if other investors later change their minds about the company's prospects. A gain is only realized when the shares are actually sold. The same analysis applies to losses; sometimes patience is the best approach.

Stocks are bought and sold (traded) in shares, often in blocks of 100 or more. Except for the initial offering, in which the company is essentially the selling party, subsequent sales are between investors. The company whose stock is being traded does not receive any part of the proceeds from such subsequent sales.

In the United States, most stocks are traded on either the New York Stock Exchange or the NASDAQ (National Association of Securities

Dealers Automated Quotations). The New York Stock Exchange is the largest market, and it includes many blue chip companies. (A blue chip is generally considered to be a very large, stable company with consistent earnings and a long history.) The NASDAQ lists many high-tech and newer businesses. In the past, stocks on the NASDAQ have tended to fluctuate more than those on the New York Stock Exchange. Beside New York, there are large stock markets in London, Paris, Tokyo and other cities around the world. Because we now live in a global economy, what happens in markets abroad often has a direct impact on American markets.

In order to get a sense of how the market is performing, investors generally look at a stock index. In this country, the three most widely followed indices are the Dow Jones Industrial Average, the Standard and Poor's 500, and the NASDAQ Composite. As explained below, each index has a somewhat different focus.

The Dow Jones Industrial Average ("DJIA" or "Dow") is an indicator of how the largest businesses in the country are doing. All of the 30 companies listed on the Dow are blue chips. Not all the companies are industrials; for example, the Dow currently includes McDonalds, Home Depot, and Walt Disney. Over time, companies are added to and deleted from the Dow. Although the Dow is probably the most widely followed index, it does not necessarily best reflect the overall market.

Many investors believe that the Standard and Poor's 500 Index (S&P 500) provides a better indication than the Dow of how the market is doing. This index of 500 companies includes a much broader range of businesses. Many of these businesses, while still very large, are not as well-known as the thirty listed on the Dow. These are the companies, however, that may comprise the bulk of a well diversified portfolio (see below). For that reason, the S&P 500's performance might be a good standard against which a trust's performance can be measured.

The NASDAQ Composite reflects the day-to-day results of all of the stocks listed on the NASDAQ exchange. As such, it is a good indicator of how high-tech and growth stocks have done. (Some NASDAQ stocks are also included in the Dow and the S&P 500.)

Stocks can be risky, and investments are not guaranteed by the government. Businesses succeed and fail. Sometimes, what was once a successful business runs into a difficult period; sometimes a formerly successful business fails. The government does not insure a stockholder's investments. While federal agencies (such as the Securities and Exchange Commission) regulate companies that are traded on the major stock exchanges, these agencies will not rescue a stockholder who has lost money.

Bonds

A bond is basically a loan. A person who is buying a new bond is loaning money to the bond's issuer for a number of years. For example, the federal government might issue a $10,000 bond which will be due in ten years. Until the bond matures, the government will pay the bond holder a fixed amount of interest twice a year. Ten years after the bond has been issued, the federal government will pay whoever happens to be holding the bond at that time $10,000. Bonds are issued by federal, state and local governments and by private corporations.

A bond issued by the United States government (a "U.S. Treasury") is generally considered to be the safest type of bond. This is because the debt is backed by the full faith and credit of the United States, and there is virtually no chance of a default. U.S. Treasuries are very easy to purchase and sell. The longest U.S. Treasuries (technically called treasury bonds) mature in 30 years; the shortest (technically called treasury bills) mature in a matter of months. A short-term, U.S. Treasury bond can sometimes serve as a substitute for cash.

Individual states, municipalities, and other government agencies can also issue bonds. These are generally called municipal bonds. Because state and local governments are not as financially secure as the federal government, municipal bonds may offer investors better interest rates than U.S. Treasuries. This is done to induce investors to purchase the bonds in the first place. Subject to some exceptions, the interest paid on municipal bonds is exempt from federal taxes. (Similarly, the interest paid on U.S. Treasuries is exempt from state and local taxes.)

Corporate bonds are issued by individual businesses. The level of risk varies greatly depending on the particular corporation. For the most part, risk is the chance that the corporation will not be able to pay the interest on the bond or pay the face value of the bond as it comes due. The riskiest corporate bonds are sometimes referred to as junk bonds. The interest rate on corporate bonds will likely be higher than that offered by either U.S. Treasuries or municipal bonds. Corporate interest is taxable at both the state and federal levels.

Because the interest rate on a given bond is fixed, its market price will be affected by changes in interest rates that occur after the bond has been issued. For example, suppose the federal government issues a long-term (30-year) bond for $10,000 that pays an annual interest rate of 4.0%. An investor buys the bond for $10,000.

If interest rates rise, the value of the bond will go down. Assume that before the bond's maturity date, interest rates rise to 6.0%. If the bondholder wants to sell his 4.0% bond, he will have to offer it at a price below the $10,000 sum he originally paid. Otherwise, a potential buyer could simply pay $10,000 to the government for a new bond that pays 6.0% interest.

If interest rates fall, the value of the bond will rise. Following along with our example, assume that interest rates fall to 2.0%. The bondholder could sell his 4.0% bond for more than $10,000. The increased price would reflect the fact that the 4.0% bond offers a substantially higher return than a current 2.0% bond.

In either case, the investor could simply continue to hold the original bond, receive the semi-annual interest payments, and, upon the bond's maturity, receive the $10,000 face value.

In general, the price of bonds, particularly government bonds, does not fluctuate as much as the price of stocks. This means that large gains or losses are more likely to be realized in the stock market than the bond market. However, in a well diversified portfolio there is a place for both stocks and bonds.

As noted, U.S. Treasuries are backed by the federal government. State and local bonds are backed by the governments (or agencies) that issued them. A third type of bonds, corporate bonds, are not backed by the government. This means that if the corporation goes bankrupt, the corporate bondholder may loose his investment. The government will not come to the rescue of a corporate bondholder.

Cash

Every trust portfolio will always include some cash. This is the money that is used to cover routine expenses. A trustee might also hold additional cash to meet anticipated purchases, such as a computer, wheelchair, or travel.

Cash can also be kept for investment purposes. This is especially true in times of financial uncertainty. Cash is considered the safest way to hold property. (For that reason, the rate of return on a cash account is often the lowest.) If a trust normally keeps five to ten percent of its property in cash, a trustee might decide to double or triple that amount during difficult economic periods. The additional cash can be raised by selling stocks or bonds. Extra cash can also come from dividend and interest payments and from bonds as they mature.

Cash is often held in a money market account at a bank or other financial institution. This type of account offers a higher interest rate than a savings or checking account. However, as explained below, money market accounts are not federally insured.

Over the long-run, holding excessive amounts of cash might not be a wise investment approach. First, the interest earned on the cash might be less than the rate of inflation. If this is the case, then the effective purchasing power of the cash is actually decreasing over time. It might not matter too much for a few months or a year. However, over a period of several years, the impact of inflation could be quite strong. Second, there is a lost opportunity cost in keeping excessive amounts of cash. Cash which could be invested for growth and income in stocks and bonds is instead only earning a relatively small amount of interest at the bank.

Checking and savings accounts that are kept at a Federal Deposit Insurance Corporation (FDIC) member bank are insured for up to $250,000. (The FDIC, which provides the insurance, is a part of the federal government.) The FDIC insures accounts at different banks separately. This means that a trustee who wanted to insure $500,000 could divide the money between two banks to reach the level of protection that he sought. The $250,000 limit will remain in effect until the end of 2013 and then drop to $100,000 in 2014.

Mutual Funds

A mutual fund pools money from many investors and then invests that money in a specific target (such as technology companies) or for a specific goal (such as low volatility). For example, as far as stocks are concerned, money could be divided among a growth fund, an income fund, and an international fund. (There are many other different types of stock funds, including those that invest primarily in large, mid-sized, or small companies.) Alternatively, an investor might choose to invest in an index fund, such as one that mirrors the S&P 500. Some funds focus primarily on bonds, and others mix stocks and bonds.

Each fund will have a manager, who is responsible for overseeing and trading the fund's investments on a regular basis. The manager and his or her staff are paid by the fund. That expense is then indirectly passed on to all the fund's investors. Funds that charge a commission are called load funds. The commission is due when the investor initially purchases shares in the fund or when the investor subsequently sells the shares.

There is a great deal of information available about mutual funds in print and on the Internet. One well-known service that provides such information is Morningstar (http://www.Morningstar.com). Individual funds are often ranked by performance over both short and long term periods. Comparisons can be made to other funds that have the same objectives. Funds can also be evaluated based on the expenses they incur or the volatility in their share price.

Mutual funds are especially attractive because they allow investors to quickly and easily diversify their investments. As a trustee, diversification should be one of your primary objectives. (This is explained below.) Another benefit of mutual funds is the professional management that comes with the investment. This is especially helpful if, like many investors, your time is limited.

Diversification

Diversification is an important investment concept. Essentially, it means spreading the risk. No matter how attractive an opportunity might seem at the outset, investments don't always work out as planned. Even the best investors sometimes get it "wrong." Diversification is a way to minimize the damage when things go wrong.

There are several ways to diversify an investment portfolio. We will look at two of them.

Diversification Among Stocks, Bonds and Cash

One level of diversification is to divide the trust's investments among stocks, bonds and cash. For example, a portfolio might consist of 60% stocks, 30% bonds, and 10% cash.

Diversification between stocks, bonds, and cash can cushion a broad decline, especially in the stock market. For example, if the market as a whole experienced a steep fall, chances are that the prices of most stocks would go down. (There are always the lucky exceptions, but those are likely to be few and far between.) In a declining market, it would be much better to have only 60% of the trust's property invested in stocks rather than 100%. To take the example a step further, if bonds perform inversely to stocks (as is sometimes the case, particularly with U.S. Treasuries) then a stock loss could be partially offset by a bond gain. Finally, the additional property that was kept as cash would further stabilize the portfolio.

The benefit of diversification does, however, come at a price. In a rising stock market it would (in retrospect) have been better to have more money invested in stocks. The problem is that few investors can predict accurately and consistently when the market is at the bottom and when it is at the top. ("Buy low, sell high" sounds great, until you actually try to do it!)

Diversification Among Industries and Companies

Diversification can also be achieved by sector (or industry) and by company. A trust's investment portfolio can be split among several different sectors. For example, approximately equal amounts might be invested in the energy, technology, financial and pharmaceutical sectors. If one particular sector experiences a dramatic decline (as happened recently with banks and other financial institutions), then the other sectors might not be as adversely affected. Again, the goal is to cushion (if not necessarily reverse) the loss.

Further diversification can be realized by investing in several different companies within each sector. This minimizes the chance that one particular company's misfortune turns into a disaster for the trust. It is better to suffer a loss from a company that consists of just two percent of the trust's portfolio than to suffer a loss from a company that consists of 20 percent of the trust's portfolio. Furthermore, a problem might be specific to just one company within a given sector. A poor management decision at one company could even work to its competitor's advantage. Again, spreading the risk reduces the loss.

Diversification is also possible with bonds. Holdings can be split between government bonds and corporate bonds. Diversification can also be realized by purchasing bonds that mature at different times. To some extent, maturity diversification reduces the risk that subsequent interest rate changes will adversely affect the value of the trust's overall bond portfolio.

Chapter 13
Closing the Trust

Eventually the special needs trust will end. If you are the trustee at that time, you will be responsible for closing the trust and distributing the remaining funds. You may be faced with competing claims from the state Medicaid agency, creditors who are owed money from the trust, and the beneficiary's relatives. This chapter explains how to resolve those claims and close the trust in an orderly and efficient manner.

Overview

In most cases, the special needs trust will end when the beneficiary with a disability dies. In a few cases, however, the trust will continue to operate for one or more successor beneficiaries. (The successor beneficiaries are the individuals or groups who will benefit from the trust when the beneficiary with a disability dies.) If that is the case with the trust you are managing, you must contact the successor beneficiaries and let them know that you are managing the trust for their benefit.

Some trustees are concerned that if the trust ends when the beneficiary dies, they will no longer have any authority to act. However, they need not be concerned. When a trust ends, the trustee remains in office for a reasonable period of time. During this "winding down" phase, the trustee can conclude the trust business and distribute the remaining funds.

Timing can be important when it comes to closing the trust. If possible, you should try to close the trust and distribute the assets as close as possible to the end of the trust's tax year. (For most trusts, this is December 31.) This will avoid having the trust extend into the next tax year.

For most trustees, closing the trust will involve the following tasks:

- Reimbursing the state Medicaid agency, if that is required.
- Paying the trust's final expenses.
- Filing the final state and federal income tax returns.
- Providing a final financial account to the beneficiaries.
- Transferring the assets to the beneficiaries.

The rest of this chapter will explain those tasks.

Reimburse the State Medicaid Agency, if Required

In some cases, the state Medicaid agency must be reimbursed from the trust funds. This will involve paying back the state for the Medicaid benefits the beneficiary received while he or she was alive. SSI benefits do not have to be repaid.

Not every trust requires reimbursement to the state. However, if the trust you are managing does require you to pay back the state, you must proceed very carefully. If the amount owed to the state is more than the remaining trust assets, the state will probably set limits on the amounts you can pay for items like the beneficiary's funeral expenses and his or her personal bills. You will need to work closely with your attorney and the state Medicaid agency to reach an agreement regarding the expenses that will be permitted. In this way, you will avoid making yourself personally liable for the state's Medicaid bill.

Find out if Medicaid Benefits Must be Repaid

You will need to find out if the remaining funds must be applied to the beneficiary's Medicaid bill. Whether Medicaid must be repaid will depend on two factors:

- The terms of the trust
- The laws of the state where the beneficiary lived at the time of his or her death

The terms of the trust. Some trusts contain a so-called Medicaid pay-back provision that requires the trustee to apply the remaining trust funds to the beneficiary's outstanding Medicaid bill. Usually only *first party trusts* contain this kind of provision. In most cases, property in a *third party trust* does not have to be repaid. (A third party trust contains assets that belonged to someone other than the beneficiary with a disability before they were put in the trust.)

The only instance when funds in a third party trust must be repaid is when a person who wants to qualify for institutional-level Medicaid benefits transfers his or her assets to a special needs trust for the benefit of a person with a disability.[20] A common situation involves an elderly parent of a son or daughter with a disability. We described such a situation in Chapter 1, "The Special Needs Trust." The parent is about to enter a nursing home and has more than $2,000 in resources. The resources prevent the parent from qualifying for Medicaid nursing home level benefits because a single person cannot have more than $2,000 in resources. The parent can transfer the excess resources to a special needs "payback" trust for the son or daughter. The parent can qualify immediately for Medicaid benefits without incurring a waiting period. When the son or daughter dies, the state is reimbursed for the son's or daughter's (not the parent's) Medicaid bill.

The laws of the state where the beneficiary resided. Even if the terms of the trust do not require Medicaid to be paid back, the laws of the state where the Medicaid recipient lived at the time of his or her death might require reimbursement.

The federal Medicaid statute (OBRA '93) permits the states to pass laws to recover their medical costs from any property in which the deceased Medicaid recipient had a legal interest at the time of his or her death. Some states have passed these kinds of laws (known as "expanded estate recovery"), and others are considering doing so. The property that can be recovered can include items like joint accounts, life insurance proceeds, annuities, and trust assets. However, the state's ability to recover its medical costs is limited. The states may only collect benefits the person received while he or she was:

- age 55 or older, or
- a permanent resident in a nursing home or other medical setting

[20] A person who lives in a rehabilitation hospital or nursing home would need institutional-level Medicaid benefits.

Your attorney can tell you how the Medicaid laws in your state apply to the trust you are managing.

Find out How Much is Owed to the State

In order to find out how much is owed to the state, you can contact the Medicaid office in the state where the beneficiary lived and received Medicaid benefits. If the beneficiary lived in more than one state, you must contact those states as well. Each state is entitled to be repaid.

Ask each Medicaid office to provide an itemized statement of charges. The statement will include items like physician care, prescription drug charges, nursing home costs, and personal care attendant services. Be sure to carefully review the statement to make sure the amounts charged for the services are reasonably accurate.

The dates of service can be important too. If the trust was funded with the proceeds of an injury settlement, the state was probably paid from the settlement funds before they were placed in the trust. Thus, you must carefully check the dates of service to make sure the medical bills do not pre-date the trust. We have occasionally seen the state make a mistake when a trust was being closed by erroneously trying to collect the same medical costs that were paid before the trust was opened.

Follow the State Procedure if There is not Enough Money to Pay the Claim

If the state's claim for reimbursement is more than the remaining trust funds, the state will adjust its claim so that you can pay some of the trust's final expenses. The particular items will vary from state to state. The state might even allow you to pay for items that are not permitted under the trust document, such as the beneficiary's funeral bill. The reason has to do with a "disconnect" between the way federal and state laws are applied. The POMS (federal Social Security guidelines) that came into effect in January 2000 prohibit the trustee from paying the beneficiary's funeral costs or personal debts before paying the state's Medicaid bill. [SI 01120.203B3a] However, when it comes to recovering Medicaid benefits, the states (applying state law) do not necessarily have to follow these restrictive guidelines. At least one state (Massachusetts) permits the trustee to pay the beneficiary's reasonable funeral costs before reimbursing the state. In short, you will have to find out which expenses the state will allow you to pay. You will also have to reach an agreement with the state as to the specific amounts. Your attorney can help you with this.

All states will permit you to pay:

- The beneficiary's state and federal income taxes, and
- Reasonable administrative costs to close the trust, such as tax preparation, bookkeeping, and trustee fees

Most states will probably *not* allow you to pay expenses like:

- Trustee fees for services you provided before the beneficiary died (This is a good reason to pay yourself at least annually, as we recommend in Chapter 8, "The Trustee.")
- The beneficiary's funeral and burial costs (See discussion above. You should consider pre-paying the beneficiary's funeral and burial costs, as we mention in Chapter 10, "Everyday Management.")
- The beneficiary's personal debts.

Obtain a Written Release

After you have reached an agreement with the state Medicaid agency, be sure to obtain a written release from the agency. If the beneficiary received benefits in more than one state, you should obtain releases from those states as well. The release should state that the agency is accepting the funds in full satisfaction of its claim. As a result, the state will no longer have any claim against the trust funds or you personally. Obtaining a release is for your protection, because if you erroneously distribute funds the state is entitled to receive, you might have to compensate the state from your personal funds.

Pay the Trust's Final Expenses

If the trust document and the pertinent state laws do not require you to pay back the state, then you do not need to be concerned about Medicaid reimbursement. You can proceed to pay the trust's final expenses. However, since each trust is different, you must carefully review the trust document to find out the specific expenses you can pay. The following are some common expenses that trustees pay before they distribute the trust funds.

Administrative Expenses to Close the Trust

You may pay reasonable fees for the services of professionals who help you conclude the trust business, such as an accountant, tax preparer, and attorney. You can also pay yourself a reasonable fee to close the trust. However, there could be a problem if you attempt to pay yourself substantial fees for services you provided to the beneficiary before he or she died, because the remainder beneficiaries could challenge your fee. This problem is discussed in Chapter 8, "The Trustee," and in the Medicaid reimbursement section of this chapter.

Administrative Expenses Incurred Before the Beneficiary Died

There may be outstanding bills for items like case management services, investment services, legal advice, and tax preparation. You should pay these kinds of expenses even if the trust does not specifically mention them.

Funeral and Burial Expenses

Many trust documents specifically permit the trustee to pay the beneficiary's funeral and burial costs. However, you should make sure that other funds have not been set aside for this purpose. For example, sometimes a life insurance policy is earmarked to pay for funeral expenses, or there might be a pre-paid funeral or burial fund. Such funds should be used first before the trust funds are spent.

If the trust document does not specifically authorize you to pay for any funeral or burial expenses, you should obtain the remainder beneficiaries' permission to pay for them. After all, these expenses are not necessarily related to the beneficiary's "special needs."

The Beneficiary's Personal Debts

The beneficiary might have outstanding personal bills for items like rent, utilities, or credit card purchases. If you customarily paid these expenses while the beneficiary was alive, you should pay the final bills.

File the Final Income Tax Returns

A trustee must file the trust's final federal and state income tax returns.

Federal Income Taxes

With federal income taxes, the procedure will depend on whether the trust is a self-funded trust or a third party trust.

- If the trust is self-funded, the procedure will not be much different from what you have done in prior years. (A self-funded trust is one that contains assets that belonged to the beneficiary before they were put into the trust.) Recall from Chapter 11, "Taxes," that a self-funded trust passes its income and losses through to the beneficiary. The trust files a so-called information return but does not pay any federal income tax. The beneficiary reports the income and losses on his or her personal income tax return. In the trust's final year of operation, all income and losses are passed through and taxed directly to the remainder beneficiaries.

- With a third party trust, you will use a different procedure for the final return than in prior years. (A third party trust is one that contains assets that belonged to someone other than the beneficiary before they were put in the trust.) In prior years, the third party trust probably paid its own taxes. Any income and losses were reported on the trust income tax return (Form 1041). In the trust's final year, the procedure is different. The trust will file a final Form 1041 that passes all income and losses through to the remainder beneficiaries. As a result, thc trust itself will not pay any federal income taxes during its final year of operation. This is true even if the trust paid its own taxes in prior years. Be sure to check the box at the top of Form 1041 that indicates it is a final return. That way, the IRS will not be contacting you in future years inquiring as to why you have not filed a return.

State Income Taxes

Each state has its own procedures for paying the trust's final state income taxes. For instance, in Massachusetts, all income is taxed to the trust, not the beneficiaries. This is true even for third party trusts that pay their own federal income taxes. Thus, in Massachusetts a trustee must use the trust funds to pay the trust's income taxes for the final year of operation. Your tax advisor or attorney can tell you if this is required in your state.

Form 56

You should file IRS Form 56 ("Notice Concerning Fiduciary Responsibility") when you close the trust. Previously we told you to file that form when you opened the trust. When you close the trust, you should file another Form 56. This time you are telling the IRS that you have closed the trust and no longer have any fiduciary responsibility. Form 56 and instructions are located in the Appendix.

Provide a Final Account to the Beneficiaries

When you close the trust you must provide a final financial account to the beneficiaries. The final account will cover the period from the end of the previous account until you close the trust and distribute the assets. You use the same basic format that you used in previous years. (The accounting procedure is described in Chapter 10, "Everyday Management.") The difference is that the final account will show the proposed distributions to the beneficiaries.

Along with the account, you should provide each beneficiary with the *tax cost basis* of any item you distribute in-kind. (In-kind distributions are discussed later in this chapter.) The tax cost basis is the amount you paid for an investment (stock, bond, mutual fund, real estate), including commissions. For real estate, the cost basis may be affected by items like depreciation, capital repairs, and capital improvements. When you sell an investment, your tax cost basis is deducted from your sale proceeds to determine your capital gain or loss. Knowing the tax cost basis will make the beneficiaries' tax reporting easier in the future when they sell the item.

We also recommend that you obtain each beneficiary's written assent (agreement) to the account. This is for your own protection. If a beneficiary has assented in writing to the account, he or she cannot challenge you later on any particular item. The written assents should be obtained before you make the final distributions. A sample Assent form is located in the Appendix.

Transfer the Trust Assets to the Beneficiaries

The final step is to distribute the remaining assets to the beneficiaries.

Create a Reserve Fund

Instead of distributing all the assets and closing the trust bank account, we recommend that you hold back a small amount of money as a reserve fund. The fund can be used to pay for any additional expenses that might come up, like income taxes or tax preparation fees. The reserve fund does not have to be large — $2,500 to $5,000 is usually sufficient, depending on the expenses you anticipate. After a year or two, or whenever you are satisfied that all trust expenses have been paid, you can close the bank account and distribute the funds to the beneficiaries. We suggest that you keep the reserve fund in a non-interest bearing account. This way, the funds will not generate any income, and you will not have to file any additional incomc tax returns. A final account that contains a reserve fund is located in Appendix 4.

Determine who will Receive the Remaining Funds

Be sure to read the trust document carefully to find out who will receive the remaining funds. Every trust is different. Some trusts state that the beneficiary may specify who will receive the remaining funds by writing a will. (This is called a *power of appointment.*) In that case, you must find out if the beneficiary exercised the power of appointment. If he or she did so, you will have to work with the personal representative of the beneficiary's estate to make sure the funds are distributed according to the instructions in his or her will.

Some trusts are subject to court review. This could be the case if the trust was created as the result of a lawsuit and the court retained supervision over the trust. If the trust you are managing is being supervised by the court, you must check the court file to see if a particular distribution of assets is required when the trust ends.

If the trust did not contain a power of appointment and there are no instructions from a court, you must distribute the funds to the remainder beneficiaries who are named in the document. These could be individuals or organizations such as charities.

What if a remainder beneficiary has died? In that case, you must carefully review the trust document to determine who will receive the deceased person's share of the trust property. The funds might pass to the person's "issue" (this legal term means the person's descendents, such as children or grandchildren), or they might pass to the surviving remainder beneficiaries.

If a remainder beneficiary is a minor child or a person with a disability, you must read the trust document to find out the proper way to distribute the beneficiary's property to him or her. Many trusts give the trustee wide latitude. For example, if the beneficiary is a minor, the trustee might be permitted to give the funds to the person's parent. Another option might be to set-up a custodial account for the child.[21] If the beneficiary has a disability, the trustee might have authority to give the funds to the person's legal guardian or conservator. Some trusts even permit the trustee to continue to hold the funds in trust for the person's benefit.

Select the Method of Transfer

Most trust documents permit the trustee to distribute the assets *in cash* or *in kind*. A cash distribution means that you sell the asset and give the sale proceeds in cash to the beneficiary. When you distribute an asset in kind, you transfer ownership of the asset directly to the person. Here are some factors to consider in deciding which method of transfer to use:

- *Type of asset.* Some assets such as cash are easy to transfer. You simply write a check to give each beneficiary their proportionate share. With a mutual fund, you can either liquidate the fund and give the proceeds to the beneficiaries (cash distribution), or instruct the company to re-register the fund so that each beneficiary receives a share (in-kind distribution). If the trust owns any real estate, it should probably be sold and the net proceeds divided among the beneficiaries. However, if the beneficiaries tell you they do not want the property to be sold, you can give a deed that transfers ownership to the beneficiaries.

[21] All the states allow someone who is holding funds for a minor to set-up an account under the Uniform Transfers to Minors Act. The funds can be managed for the person until he reaches the age specified in the statute (18 in some states, 21 in others).

- ***Tax considerations.*** The sale of an asset such as a stock, bond, or mutual fund is a taxable event. A capital gain or loss can occur on the sale. As we explained earlier in this chapter, for federal tax purposes, these gains and losses are passed through to the remainder beneficiaries in the final year of the trust. The beneficiaries will report them on their personal income tax returns. It might be preferable to avoid any tax consequences for the beneficiaries by transferring the assets to them in kind. If you do so, you should provide each beneficiary with the tax cost basis of the item you are transferring. (The tax cost basis was explained earlier in this chapter.) The beneficiary will need this information when he or she sells the item. If the beneficiary is a charity, taxes are not usually a concern, because most charitable organizations do not pay income taxes.

- ***The beneficiaries' preferences.*** You should contact the beneficiaries to find out their preferences. Perhaps a beneficiary might want a particular item of trust property such as a car, work of art, or furniture. When you distribute the item to that person, you must value the item and offset it against the assets the other beneficiaries receive. Conversely, a beneficiary might not want a particular item. In that case, the beneficiary could receive an equivalent amount of cash or other property.

Chapter 14
Getting Help

Every trustee brings his or her unique skills to the role. Perhaps you have a background in law and understand public benefits. Or maybe you excel in investments. Or perhaps you are a relative or close friend of the beneficiary and know his or her needs best. Whatever your special qualifications are, you will use them to further the interests of the trust and the beneficiary. Nevertheless, the trust may need services that you are not qualified to provide. In that case, you should hire someone to assist you. Most trust documents authorize you to obtain professional assistance, and some even encourage you to do so. This chapter explains the services that attorneys, financial advisers, tax professionals, social workers, and case managers can provide. We also provide advice on how to locate these professionals and evaluate their qualifications.

Attorneys

Almost every trustee can benefit from working with an attorney at one time or another. We recommend that you hire an attorney when you first take over managing the trust. That way, there will be someone to call whenever questions come up. The attorney you hire does not need to be the same attorney who wrote the trust. However, the person should be an expert in special needs trusts and public benefits.

Services

When you open the trust or take over an existing trust, your attorney can:

- Review the public benefits the beneficiary receives and explain the pertinent rules of those programs.

- Help you obtain an Employer Identification Number (EIN) for the trust.

- Review the trust document and explain your fiduciary responsibilities, including any local rules in your state.

- Tell you how to spend money from the trust in ways that will not reduce the beneficiary's public assistance.

- Show you how to open bank accounts and register assets in the name of the trust.

- Tell you which state's laws govern the trust and explain any special requirements under that state's laws, including the Uniform Prudent Investor Act and the Uniform Trust Code (if the state has passed some version of these laws).

- Prepare any necessary Trustee Acceptance or Resignation forms.

- Help you set your trustee fee according to the standards in your area.

On an ongoing basis, the attorney can:

- Explain your fiduciary duties.

- Tell you about any changes in the law that may affect the trust. (For example, as a result of an important change to SSI in 2005, a recipient's benefit will not be affected if he or she receives a gift of clothing.)

- Help you resolve any conflicts of interest that may come up between you and beneficiaries.

- Help you prepare the annual financial accounts and give proper legal notice to the beneficiaries.

- Advise you how to respond to any notices the beneficiary (or you, as his or her legal representative) might receive from any agency that provides assistance, such as Social Security, Medicaid, or the local housing authority.

- Prepare any caregiver agreements or employment contracts for people who provide services to the beneficiary.

- Advise you about withholding for FICA (Social Security) taxes, state unemployment laws, and workers compensation requirements for any employees you hire to take care of the beneficiary.

- Advise you on the best way to own any assets that the trust purchases for the beneficiary, such as a home or vehicle.

- Assist you with the purchase or sale of real estate.

- Put you in touch with other professionals who can assist you, such as a tax professional to prepare and file income tax returns or a financial adviser to assist with investments.

When you close the trust, the attorney can:

- Prepare the final account and obtain the beneficiaries' written assents.

- If there is any court involvement, obtain court approval of your final account so that you will be released from any personal liability.

- If you are managing a "payback" trust, review the state's claim for medical services, determine whether the charges are proper, pay the correct amount due, and obtain a release.

- If there are any funds left in the trust after the state has been paid, determine who will receive the remaining assets, and advise you on the proper way to distribute them.

Locating an Attorney

The attorney you hire should be an expert in special needs trusts and public benefits. How can you locate such a person? Perhaps you have a friend or relative who is an attorney, or maybe you have worked with an attorney in the past. If so, that person may be able to recommend someone. In addition, most local advocacy organizations and bar associations maintain referral lists of attorneys who specialize in disability matters. You can also obtain a referral from the National Academy of Elder Law Attorneys (http://naela.com), which has chapters in every state. Some NAELA attorneys specialize in disability law.

Once you have obtained some referrals, call two or three of the attorneys. Ask about their experience and fees. Then select one and set-up a meeting to review the trust and answer your questions. Some attorneys charge a flat fee for an initial consultation fee, while others charge by the hour. However, if you simply want to interview the person, some attorneys do not charge anything for a brief "get acquainted" meeting.

Financial Advisers

If you are not knowledgeable about investments, you should hire a financial adviser, or at least consult with someone when you take over managing the trust. The Uniform Prudent Investor Act, which most states have adopted, requires a trustee to review the trust assets and decide which ones to keep and which ones to dispose of. This must be done within a reasonable period of time after accepting the trusteeship or receiving the trust assets. [Uniform Prudent Investor Act, section 5] A financial adviser can help you with this task.

The following are some other services a financial adviser can offer:

- Help you budget the trust funds so you will know how much you can afford to spend each year.

- Advise you on the proper allocation of investments for the trust (stocks, bonds, cash, etc.). This is important because the trust assets must earn a reasonable rate of return without incurring undue risk.

- Recommend particular stocks or mutual funds.

- Take over investing the trust funds through a managed account.

- Help you manage the cash flow among the different investment accounts. In that way, you only keep a minimum amount of money in a non-interest bearing checking account. When you need more money, you can transfer it from a higher yield money market or investment account.

Selecting a Financial Adviser

How can you know if the person you are considering hiring is qualified and will do a good job? There is no magic formula. However, in order to meet your fiduciary responsibilities, you must exercise care in selecting the person. We recommend that you meet with two or three firms or individuals before hiring someone. Make sure the person and his or her firm are registered or licensed. This is very important, because if you hand your money over to an unregistered adviser who later goes out of business, you may have no recourse. You should also check for any pending or past disciplinary proceedings. The following are some specific steps you can take:

- Assess the person's experience and credentials. The person you hire should have at least five years' experience and have one or more professional designations, such as Certified Financial Planner. These individuals are licensed by the Certified Financial Planner Board, a national group that sets high standards for its members. You can check out whether the person has had any complaints lodged against him or her by going to the Board's website, http://www.cfp-net.

- Review state registrations and any history of discipline. Investment advisers who manage assets of $25 million or more must register with the Securities and Exchange Commission (SEC). Most states also require advisers who manage less than that amount to register. You can check the person's status, including any disciplinary proceedings, by going to http://www.nasaa.org. This is the website of the North American Securities Administrators Association, which will direct you to your state's regulatory agency.

- Request a copy of the adviser's ADV. The ADV is a standard form application that every registered adviser must file with the SEC. It provides detailed information about the person's operation, background, conflicts of interest, and disciplinary background. The ADVs for financial services firms are available on the SEC website (http://adviserinfo.sec.gov).

Tax Advisers

When you invest the trust property, it will probably produce interest, dividends, and capital gains. This income must be reported on the trust's federal and state income tax returns. This is true even if the trust "passes through" its income to the beneficiary. You will need a tax professional to assist you.

The following are some services a tax professional can provide:

- Prepare annual state and federal income tax returns, including Schedule K-1 forms that list the beneficiary's share of taxable income and deductions.

- Advise you whether the trust must pay any estimated income taxes, and if so, prepare the necessary paperwork.

- Respond to any notices you receive from federal or state tax authorities.

- Work with your financial adviser to determine which assets to retain and which ones to sell in order to obtain the most favorable tax treatment.

- Help you determine the tax cost basis for the trust assets. If you sell a trust asset, you must know its cost basis in order to compute the capital gain. If you distribute any assets in-kind to the beneficiaries when you close the trust, you should tell them the tax cost basis of the asset. (See Chapter 13, "Closing the Trust.")

- Assist you with items like income tax withholding, Medicare withholding, and state workers' compensation insurance for any employees you hire.

Choosing a Tax Adviser

When it comes to selecting a tax adviser, the person's qualifications are important. Make sure the person is experienced in preparing trust income tax returns. Many tax preparers, including most chain franchises, do not have the necessary experience. We recommend that you hire an accountant or certified public accountant (CPA). A CPA is a college graduate who has passed a comprehensive exam. Your attorney or financial planner can probably refer you to a qualified person. Before you hire the tax adviser, be sure to ask about his or her fees. In our experience, there can be a wide range of fees that tax professionals charge.

Legal Aid and Advocacy Organizations

If the beneficiary needs any legal services that are not related to the trust, a local legal aid office or advocacy group may be able to provide them. These publicly funded organizations can provide a wide range of legal services at free or reduced cost to low income people. The beneficiary must disclose the existence of the special needs trust in case that would affect his or her financial eligibility for services. Some organizations provide services to individuals who reside within a specific geographic area. Many law schools operate free legal clinics for eligible individuals. The following are some of the services that legal aid and advocacy organizations can provide:

- Representing a person in public housing matters, including rent setting proceedings and evictions.
- Helping a person obtain public benefits such as SSI or SSDI, and appeal a denial of benefits.
- Obtaining state-funded services for individuals with intellectual disabilities, mental illness, or physical disabilities.
- Assisting a person to obtain a restraining order against an abusive spouse or partner.
- Representing a person who is mentally ill in a civil commitment proceeding.
- Helping a person obtain food stamps or fuel assistance, or appeal a denial of assistance.
- Appealing a termination or reduction of public benefits.

The best way to locate a legal aid organization is through the Internet or the local telephone book. If the beneficiary has a case manager (see below), he or she may be able to help locate some resources.

Social Workers and Case Managers

Different beneficiaries need varying degrees of help. Their needs can also change over time. An experienced case manager can be very useful, especially if the beneficiary does not have any close family members who are involved with his or her care. Even if the trust has a large amount of money, it will not do the beneficiary much good if it is not used or — most importantly — used well. A good case manager can be your eyes and ears. He or she can:

- Oversee the person's general well-being and make sure that his or her needs for housing, socialization, food, and medical care are being met.
- Assist the person with routine paperwork such as applications, public benefit reviews, leases, vouchers, etc.
- Make sure the person gets up in the morning and help organize his or her day.
- Help the person find an apartment or buy a car.
- Teach the person how to use public transportation.
- Help manage the person's finances, including deposit income checks, write checks to pay bills, and balance the checkbook.
- Help with meal planning, food shopping, and buying personal items.
- Assist the person with laundry and keeping his or her home reasonably clean and neat.
- Help the person obtain his or her medications and make sure they are being taken.

- Set-up medical appointments and make sure the person attends them.

- Coordinate the person's medical care among the different providers.

- Teach the person how to respond to an emergency, such as a fire, break-in, or medical emergency, or assist the person if an emergency occurs.

- Locate Personal Care Attendants and others who can help the beneficiary with routine daily care.

Locating a Social Worker or Case Manager

If the person receives any assistance from the state, he or she may already have a case manager. If not, you can find a private social worker or case manager through an organization such as The Arc (formerly called the Association for Retarded Citizens). The Arc has chapters in every state. Your local chapter of a national disability organization (National Alliance for the Mentally Ill, United Cerebral Palsy, Muscular Dystrophy Association, etc.) might also be able to help you identify someone. Information on these organizations is located in Chapter 16, "Resources."

Chapter 15
Glossary of Terms

Account/Accounting: A summary of financial activity for a trust for a specific period of time, usually one year.

Administrative expenses: The costs associated with operating a trust, such as attorney fees, trustee fees, bookkeeping costs, accounting expenses, filing fees, etc.

Annuity: A contract sold by an insurance company that makes payments to the owner at specified intervals.

Assent: Agreement. The beneficiary of a trust can assent to certain actions by the trustee.

Asset: Same as resource.

Beneficiary: The person a trust is intended to benefit.

Capital gain: The amount by which an asset's selling price exceeds its initial purchase price.

Child: A person under age 18.

Code of Federal Regulations (CFR): A collection of the rules and requirements of the federal government. For instance, the Department of Housing and Urban Development (HUD) enacts regulations about rental assistance programs and publishes them in the Code of Federal Regulations.

Co-trustee: A person who manages a trust with another trustee.

Countable Asset: A resource (item of value) that is included when determining if a person can qualify for a public benefit program.

Corpus: The assets of a trust, also called the principal of the trust.

Cost basis: The amount paid for an investment (stock, bond, mutual fund), including commissions. With real estate, the cost basis may be affected by items like depreciation, capital repairs, and capital improvements.

Disability: As defined by the Social Security Administration in the SSI and SSDI Programs, for an adult, "the inability to engage in substantial gainful activity due to a medical impairments or combination of impairments that can be expected to last for a continuous period of twelve months or result in death."

Distribution: A payment made by a trustee of a trust. The trustee can distribute funds to the beneficiary or to a person who has provided goods and services to the beneficiary or to the trust.

Donor: The person who creates a trust. A donor is sometimes called a declarant, grantor, settlor, or trustor.

Earned Income: Income that is earned from one's labor.

Federal benefit rate (FBR): The amount the federal government contributes to an individual's SSI grant. In 2010, the amount is $674 per month. Many states supplement the federal benefit rate, which results in larger payments for SSI recipients in those states.

Fiduciary: A person or organization that has a duty to act exclusively for another person's benefit. A trustee is a fiduciary.

Grantor: The creator of a trust. The grantor is sometimes called the declarant, donor, settlor, or trustor.

HUD: The Department of Housing and Urban Development, which manages housing assistance programs like Section 8.

Impairment-Related Work Expenses (IRWE): Certain items that are needed by a person with a disability in order to work, such as special shoes, specialized transportation, or job supervision.

Independent Trustee: A trustee who is not under the control of a beneficiary of a trust and who cannot receive any benefits from the trust.

In-Kind Income: As used in public benefit programs, food or shelter, or something a recipient can use to obtain food or shelter.

Irrevocable Trust: A trust that does not permit the grantor to take back the trust property.

Medicaid: A federal and state funded health insurance program for low- and middle-income individuals and their families and for persons with disabilities.

Medicare: The health insurance program associated with Social Security. Medicare is funded by the federal government.

OBRA'93: The Omnibus Budget Reconciliation Act of 1993, which is located at 24 U.S.C. 1396p(d)(4)(A). This federal statute authorized the special needs "payback" trust. A person with a disability who transfers his assets to a special needs payback trust can qualify for the SSI, Medicaid, subsidized housing, and other benefit programs that are based on need.

PASS (Plan for Achieving Self-Support): A program that will allow an SSI recipient to earn more income or own more assets than normally would be allowed by the program as a means to achieve self-support. A PASS must be pre-approved by the Social Security Administration.

Payback trust: A special needs trust that provides that when the beneficiary with a disability dies, the remaining trust funds will be used to reimburse the state for beneficiary's Medicaid costs. A payback trust is sometimes referred to as a "(d)(4)A trust" or an "OBRA '93 trust."

POMS (Program Operations Manual System): Guidelines that are used by the Social Security Administration to interpret its programs. The POMS are located online at http://ssa.gov.

Portfolio: A collection of stocks, bonds, mutual funds, etc.

Power of appointment: In the context of a trust, the beneficiary's ability to say who will receive the remaining trust assets after the beneficiary's death. The beneficiary exercises the power of appointment by writing a will.

Principal: The capital (or corpus) of a trust, in contrast to the income (interest, dividends, rents, etc.) the principal earns when it is invested.

Remainder beneficiary: The person who will receive the trust property after the beneficiary with a disability has died.

Revocable Trust: A trust that permits the grantor to cancel it and take back the trust property.

Resource: An item of value owned by an SSI recipient, including money, stocks, bonds, real estate, personal property, etc. SSI classifies resources as either countable or non-countable. One can have only $2,000 in countable resources to receive SSI. In this book, we use the term "asset" and "resource" interchangeably.

Section 8: A rental assistance program sponsored by HUD and managed by local housing authorities. A participant pays rent based on his or her income, and the housing authority pays the balance of the rent to the landlord.

Settlor: Same as donor or grantor.

Social Security Administration (SSA): The federal agency that manages the SSI and SSDI programs.

Special Needs Trust: A trust that holds funds for the benefit of a person with a disability. The purpose of the trust is to allow a person to receive public benefits and still have a source of funds to pay for items and services that public benefit programs do not provide.

SSDI (Social Security Disability Insurance): A federal program that pays monthly cash benefits to workers with disabilities (and their dependents) who have paid Social Security taxes on their earnings.

SSI (Supplemental Security Income): A federal benefit program that pays monthly cash benefits to individuals who are elderly, blind, or have disabilities, and who have limited income and few financial resources.

Substantial Gainful Activity (SGA): Social Security uses the term "substantial gainful activity" to determine if work is substantial enough to make a person ineligible for benefits. In 2010, a non-blind person is considered to be engaging in SGA if he or she earns more than $1,000 per month and has no deductible work-related expenses. A blind person can earn up to $1,640 before he or she is deemed to be ineligible for benefits.

Successor Beneficiary: The person(s) who benefit from the trust when the beneficiary with a disability is no longer living.

Successor Trustee: A trustee who serves when the initial trustee or trustees are no longer serving.

Supplemental Needs Trust: Same as special needs trust.

Tax cost basis: same as cost basis.

Trust: A legal arrangement in which an individual or organization gives property to a trustee to manage for one or more beneficiaries.

Trustee: The person or organization (bank, trust company, charitable corporation, etc.) that manages a trust.

Unearned Income: Income that is not derived from one's labor, such as interest, dividends, rents, royalties, alimony, etc. Any cash in excess of $20 per month that the trustee distributes to the beneficiary is considered to be unearned income under the SSI program.

Chapter 16
Resources

The resources in this chapter can assist readers who want more information on the topics in this book.

Government Websites

www.ssa.gov
The Social Security website contains the POMS (the guidelines for the Social Security programs) as well as useful information on SSI, SSDI, employment, etc.

www.irs.gov
The website of the Internal Revenue Service. You can apply for an Employer Identification Number here.

www.cms.hhs.gov
The website of the Center for Medicare and Medicaid services contains information on the Medicare and Medicaid programs.

www.medicare.gov
The government website for people with Medicare contains the annual costs, premiums, etc.

www.fedstats.gov
Contains federal statistics, including current federal poverty levels.

www.huduser.org
The website of the U.S. Department of Housing and Urban Development (HUD) contains the Section 8 income limits and the Section 8 fair market rents for all areas of the country.

Publications

An Advocate's Guide to Surviving the SSI System. Linda L. Landry, et al. Also known as "The Yellow Book," this award-winning, comprehensive resource clarifies the SSI program and focuses on eligibility for SSI benefits. Although the book has not been updated since 2002, it is still a valuable resource. $15. Order from Massachusetts Continuing Legal Education, http:// www.mcle.org.

Benefits Management for Working People with Disabilities. This 210-page reference book is considered by many to be the definitive work on SSI and SSDI work incentives and related issues. Published by Neighborhood Legal Services. $70. Can be ordered on NLS website, http://www.nls.org.

Investing and Managing Trusts under the New Prudent Investor Rule. John Train and Thomas A. Melfe, Harvard Business School Press, 1999. Directed to attorneys and professional trustees, this book explains how trustees can comply with the Prudent Investor Act.

Loring: A Trustee's Handbook. Charles E. Rounds, Jr., and Charles E. Rounds III, Aspen Publishers, Inc., 2009. Useful, one-volume handbook on trust administration.

The Only Investment Guide You'll Ever Need. Andrew Tobias, Harcourt Books, 2005. Useful, engaging guide to personal investing.

The Red Book on Employment. Publication 64-030 of the Social Security Administration: Guide to Social Security Work-related Rules and Regulations. This useful guide can be found on the SSA website http://www.ssa.gov, ordered by mail, or ordered by telephone (800-722-1213).

Section 8 Made Simple. Technical Assistance Collaborative, Inc., 2003. This excellent reader-friendly guide to the Section 8 program can be obtained free of charge from the TAC website, http://www.tacinc.org.

Organizations

These organizations may be able to help you locate an attorney, financial planner, or case manager in your area.

Academy of Special Needs Planners
http://www.specialneedsplanners.com
866-296-5509
A national network of attorneys who focus their practices on special needs planning.

The Arc of the United States
http://www.thearc.org
800-433-5255
The Arc is a community-based organization that advocates for people with intellectual and developmental disabilities.

Certified Financial Planner Board of Standards, Inc.
http://www.cfp.net
800-487-1497
This organization can help you locate a certified financial planner in your area.

Jewish Family & Children's Service
A non-denominational social service organization that provides services to individuals with disabilities and others. There are chapters in many states. To find a local chapter, search "Jewish Family & Children's Service" on the Internet.

National Academy of Elder Law Attorneys
http://www.naela.org
703-942-5711
NAELA is a national organization of attorneys who specialize in elder law. NAELA has chapters in every state. Many NAELA members also work with special needs trusts.

National Alliance for the Mentally Ill
http://www.nami.org
800-950-6264
NAMI is the nation's largest grassroots mental health organization. It is dedicated to improving the lives of individuals and families affected by mental illness.

Special Needs Alliance
http://www.specialneedsalliance.org
877-572-8472
A national group of disability and public benefit attorneys.

United Cerebral Palsy
http://www.ucp.org
800-872-5827
The mission of United Cerebral Palsy is to advance the independence, productivity, and full citizenship of people with disabilities through an affiliate network.

Appendix I

List of States that have Adopted the Uniform Trust Code

The Uniform Trust Code is a model statute. According to the National Conference of Commissioners on Uniform State Laws that drafted and approved the statute in 2004, the intent was to provide uniformity in all states in matters of trust management. As of 2009, twenty-nine states and the District of Columbia have adopted some version of the law.

If you are a trustee, it is important to know if your state has enacted some version of the Uniform Trust Code. The law may influence some of the ways you manage the trust. The UTC covers items like:

- Whether you have to provide financial accounts (reports) to the beneficiaries, and if so, how often and to which beneficiaries (including those who only have a remote interest in the trust)

- Which state's laws govern the trust, and how to change the state where the trust is managed and whose laws will govern

- The ability of creditors to obtain payment from the trust for debts owed by the grantor (creator) and the beneficiaries

The model statute contains extensive comments on each section that may not be available in the state law. The comments may be useful to attorneys and others who need additional guidance.

The Uniform Trust Code is available on the Internet at http://www.utcproject.org

The follwing is a list of states that have adopted the Uniform Trust Code and the section of each state's laws where the Code is located.

1. Alabama Ala. Code §§ 19-3B-101–19-3B-1305
2. Arizona Ariz. Trust Code 14-10101 to 14-10102
3. Arkansas Ark. Code Ann. §§ 28-73-101–28-73-1106
4. District of Columbia D.C. Code § 19-1301.01–19-1311.03
5. Florida Fla. Stat. §§ 736.0101–736.1303
6. Kansas Kan. Stat. Ann. §§ 58a-101–58a-1107
7. Maine Me. Rev. Stat. Ann. tit. 18-B, §§ 101–1104
8. Missouri Mo. Rev. Stat. §§ 456.1-101–456.11-1106
9. Nebraska Neb. Rev. Stat. §§ 30-3801–30-38,110
10. New Hampshire N.H. Rev. Stat. Ann. §§ 564-B:l 101–564-B:11-1104
11. New Mexico N.M. Stat. Ann. §§ 46A-1-101–46A-11-1104
12. North Carolina N.C. Gen. Stat. §§ 36C-1-101–36C-11-1103
13. North Dakota N.D. Cent. Code §§ 59-09-01–59-19-02
14. Ohio Ohio Rev. Code Ann. §§ 5801.01–5811.03
15. Oregon Or. Rev. Stat. §§ 130.001–130.910
16. Pennsylvania 20 Pa. Cons. Stat §§ 7701–7799.3
17. South Carolina S.C. Code Ann. §§ 62-7-101–62-7-1106
18. Tennessee Tenn. Code Ann §§ 35-15-101–35-15-1103
19. Utah Utah Code Ann §§ 75-7-101–75-7-1201
20. Virginia Va. Code Ann. §§ 55-541.01–55-551.06
21. Wyoming Wyo. Stat. Ann. §§ 4-10-101–4-10-1103

Appendix 2

List of States that have Adopted the Uniform Prudent Investor Act

The Uniform Prudent Investor Act is a model statute that governs investments by trustees. As of 2009, forty-one states and the District of Columbia have adopted the entire Act. Eight states have adopted parts of the Act.

If you are a trustee, it is important to review your state's Prudent Investor Act (or have your attorney do so). The law may require you to invest the trust funds in certain ways or limit your ability to make certain kinds of investments.

The model statute contains comments on each section that may not be available in the state law. The comments may be useful to attorneys and others who need additional guidance. The Prudent Investor Act is available on the Internet at http://www.ulaw.upenn.edu/bll/achives.ulc/uta.

List of States that have Adopted the Complete Uniform Prudent Investor Act and the section of each state's law where the Code is located.

1. Alaska AS §§ 13.36.200 to 13.36.275
2. Arizona West's Ariz. Rev. Stat. Ann §§ 14-7601 to 14-7611
3. Arkansas A.C.A. §§ 24-3-417 to 24-3-426
4. California West's Ann. Ca. Probate Code, §§ 16045 to 16054
5. Colorado West's C.S.R.A. §§ 15-1.11-101 to 15-1.1-115
6. Connecticut C.G.S.A. §§ 45a541 to 45a-541/
7. District of Columbia D.C. Code 1981 §§ 28-4701 to 28-4712
8. Hawaii H.R.S. §§ 554C-1 to 554C-12
9. Idaho I.C. §§ 68-501 to 68-514
10. Illinois West's 760 ILL Comp. Stat. §§ 5/5 and 5/5.1
11. Indiana West's A.I.C. §§ 30-4.3.5-1 to 30-4-3.5-13
12. Iowa West's Iowa Code Ann. § 633.4301 to 633.4310
13. Kansas (a) West's Kan. Stat. Ann. § 17-5004
14. Maine West's Me. Rev. Stat. Ann. Tit. 18-A, § 7-302, 7-302 note
15. Maryland West's Md. Code Ann., Est. & Trusts § 15-114
16. Massachusetts M.G.L.A. c. 203C, §§ 1-11
17. Michigan M.C.L.A. §§700.1501 to 700.1512
18. Minnesota West's Minn. Stat. Ann. §501B.151, 501B.152
19. Missouri West's Mo. Ann. Stat. §§ 456.900 to 456.913
20. Montana West's Mont. Code Ann. § 72-34-114
21. Nebraska R.R.S. 1943, §§ 8-2201 to 8-2213
22. Nevada West's Nev. Rev. Stat. § 164-050
23. New Hampshire RSA 564 A:3:B
24. New Jersey West's N.J. Stat. Ann. §3b:20-11.1 to 3B:20-11.12
25. New Mexico West's N.M. Stat. Ann. §§ 45-7-601 to 45-7-612
26. North Carolina G.S. §§ 36A-161 to 36A-173
27. North Dakota West's N.D. Cent. Code §59-02-08.1 to 59-02-08.11
28. Ohio R.C. §§ 1339.52 to 1339.61
29. Oklahoma West's 60 Okla. Stat. Ann. tit. 60§§ 175.60 to 175.72
30. Oregon West's Or. Rev. Stat. § 128.192 to 128.218
31. Pennsylvania 20 Pa. C.S.A. §§ 7201 to 7214

32. Rhode Island Gen. Laws 1956, §§ 18-15-1 to 18-15-13
33. South Carolina West's S.C. Code Ann. §62-7-302
34. Tennessee Tenn. Code Ann. 35-14-101 to 35-14-114
35. Texas West's Tex Prop. Code Ann. §75-7-302
36. Utah West's Utah Code Ann. §75-7-302
37. Vermont 9 V.S.A. §§ 4651 to 4662
38. Virginia West's Va. Code Ann. § 26-45.3 to 26-45.14
39. Washington West's Wash. Rev. Code Ann. §11.100.010 et. seq.
40. West Virginia Code, 44-6C-1 to 44-6C-15
41. Wisconsin c. 881.01 to 881.01(13)
42. Wyoming Wyo. Stat. Ann. §§ 4-9-101 to 4-9-113

List of states that have Adopted Some Form of the Uniform Prudent Investor Act and the section of each state's law where the Code is located.

1. Alabama West's Ala. Code §19-3-120.2
2. Delaware West's Del. Code Ann. tit. 12 §3302
3. Florida West's F.S.A. §§ 518.11 and 518.11
4. Georgia West's Ga. Code Ann §53-12-280
5. Kentucky Revised Statutes 287.277
6. Mississippi 91-9-601 to 91-9-627
7. New York West's N.Y. Est. Powers and Trusts Law §11-2.3
8. South Dakota West's S.D. Codified Laws Ann. §55-506

The only state that has not adopted some form of the Uniform Prudent Investor Act is Louisiana.

Appendix 3
Sample Accounts and Assent Form

In most states, a trustee must provide regular financial accounts to the beneficiary. There is no specific format that must be followed. We provide two sample accounts that a trustee can use as a guide. There is also a form for the beneficiary to sign assenting to the trustee's account.

Example of a Trustee's Annual Account

Example of a Trustee's Final Account with a Reserve Fund

Example of a Beneficiary's Assent to Trustee's Account

Example of a Trustee's Annual Account

Second Account of Sally Smith as
Trustee of the Jane Johnson Special Needs Trust
January 1, 2007, to December 31, 2007

Schedule A
Income

Number	Date	Description of Income	Amount
1		Beginning balance	$140,190
2		Interest on Eastern Bank Account #12345	$1,201
3		Vanguard Index Bond Fund #09876	$2,103
4		Monthly Payments on Promissory note owned by the trust (12 x $575.88)	$6,901
TOTAL			**$150,395**

Schedule B
Payments

Number	Date	Payee/Purpose	Amount
1	01/15/07	Jane Johnson - distribution	$1,500
2	02/01/07	Jane Johnson - distribution - clothes	$525
3	04/06/07	IRS - 2006 Income Tax	$776
4	04/05/07	Commonwealth of Mass. - 2006 Tax	$95
5	04/15/07	IRS - 2007 estimated payment	$200

6	05/25/07	Sally Smith, trustee - trustee fee	$1,500
7	05/25/07	Michael Smith - tax preparation	$250
8	07/27/07	Alternative Leisure – summer vacation for Jane Johnson	$2,250
9	12/10/07	Jane Johnson – distribution – holiday gifts	$250
TOTAL			**$7,346**

Schedule C

1. Schedule A	$150,395
2. Schedule B	$7,346
3. Schedule C	$143,049

Reconciliation – balances as of 12/31/07

Eastern Bank Money Market Acct. #12345	$74,210
Vanguard Index Bond Fund #09876	$57,939
Promissory note to John Johnson	$10,900
TOTAL	**$143,049**

Example of a Trustee's Final Account with a Reserve Fund

Final Account of Edward Jones as
Trustee of the Robert Smith Special Needs Trust
Period from August 1, 2007 to July 31, 2008

Schedule A
Income

1. Balance from prior account		$245,662
2. Interest		
Citizens Bank Estate Account	$4,101	
Central Bank Savings Account	$253	
Charles Schwab Cash Account	$2,703	
Central Bank CD	$149	
TOTAL		$7,206
3. Dividends		
Vanguard Wellesley Fund	$4,081	
Vanguard Index 500 Fund	$3,050	
AT&T	$297	
TOTAL		$7,428
4. Miscellaneous		
Federal Income Tax Refund (2006)	$870	
TOTAL		$870
TOTAL Schedule A		**$261,166**

Schedule B
Expenses

1. Funeral		
Jones Funeral Home	$8,827	
Sally Johnson - Reimburse food	$150	
Sands Monuments - headstone	$346	
TOTAL		$9,323
2. Administration		
Trustee fee	$3,250	
Tax preparation	$750	
Wire fees	$40	
TOTAL		$4,040
3. Utilities		
Cable TV/Internet	$1,800	
Telephone	$468	
TOTAL		$2,268
4. Taxes		
Federal 2007 fiduciary income taxes	$2,063	
Mass. 2007 fiduciary income taxes	$1,158	
Federal Est. 2008 fiduciary income taxes	$1,030	
Mass. Est. 2008 fiduciary income taxes	$560	
TOTAL		$4,811
5. Miscellaneous		
Middlesex Home Care	$2,700	
Attendant care services	$1,950	
Counseling	$725	
Medical co-payments and prescription drugs	$300	
TOTAL		$5,675

6. Preliminary Distributions		
John Johnson	$112,524	
David Johnson	$112,525	
TOTAL		$225,049
7. Reserve fund		$10,000*
TOTAL Schedule B		**$261,166**

<u>Schedule C</u>

Schedule A	$261,166
Schedule B	$261,166
Schedule C	**none**

*The funds will be held in reserve by the trustee in a non-interest bearing account for a period of time up to three years. The funds will be used to pay tax preparation fees for 2008, federal income taxes, state income taxes, trustee fees, and miscellaneous additional costs to the close the trust. Any remaining funds will be divided equally between John Johnson and David Johnson.

Example of a Beneficiary's Assent to Trustee's Account

The Robert Smith Special Needs Trust
Assent to the Trustee's Account

In the matter of the Robert Smith Special Needs Trust, I___________,
(name)
of______________, a party interested in the above matter, approve the
(address)
___________________________ Account of the Trustee for the period
(number of the account)
from ______________________ to _______________________.
(dates the account covers)

Date: _____________

__________________________ ________________________________
Witness Signature

Appendix 4
Sample Trustee Forms

Appendix 4 contains examples of forms the trustee can use to accept the trusteeship, resign from the trusteeship, or decline to serve as the trustee.

Example of a Trustee's Acceptance

Example of a Trustee's Resignation

Example of a Trustee's Declination

Example of a Trustee's Acceptance

The John Smith Special Needs Trust
Acceptance

I, ______________________, of ______________________________,
(name) (address)
being the designated trustee of the above captioned trust, a trust instrument dated ______________, hereby accept the appointment as trustee of that trust.

Date: ________________

____
Signature

State of ______________________________

County of ___________________________

On this _____ day of ___________, 201__, before me, the undersigned notary, personally appeared ___________________________, ______ personally known to me, or ________ proved to me through satisfactory evidence of identification, which was ________________ a driver's license ______________(other:) ________________________ ________, to be the person whose name is signed on the preceding or attached document, and who swore or affirmed to me that the contents of the document are truthful and accurate to the best of his/her knowledge and ability, and that s/he signed the document voluntarily for its stated purpose.

____
Notary Public
My Commission Expires

Example of a Trustee's Resignation

The John Smith Special Needs Trust
Resignation

I, ______________________, of ______________________________,
(name) (address)
being the trustee of the John Smith Special Needs Trust, created on ______________, hereby resign from my office as trustee.

Date: ______________

____
Signature

State of ________________________________

County of ______________________________

On this _____ day of _________ , 201 , before me, the undersigned notary, personally appeared ____________________________, ______ personally known to me, or ________ proved to me through satisfactory evidence of identification, which was _______________ a driver's license _____________(other:) ________________________ ________, to be the person whose name is signed on the preceding or attached document, and who swore or affirmed to me that the contents of the document are truthful and accurate to the best of his/her knowledge and ability, and that s/he signed the document voluntarily for its stated purpose.

____
Notary Public
My Commission Expires

Example of a Trustee's Declination

The John Smith Special Needs Trust

Declination

I, ______________________, of ________________________________,
(name) (address)
being the designated trustee of the John Smith Special Needs Trust, created on______________, hereby decline to serve.

Date: ______________

____
Signature

State of ________________________________

County of ____________________________

On this _____ day of ___________, 201__, before me, the undersigned notary, personally appeared ____________________________, ______ personally known to me, or ________ proved to me through satisfactory evidence of identification, which was _______________ a driver's license _____________(other:) _________________________ ________, to be the person whose name is signed on the preceding or attached document, and who swore or affirmed to me that the contents of the document are truthful and accurate to the best of his/her knowledge and ability, and that s/he signed the document voluntarily for its stated purpose.

____
Notary Public
My Commission Expires

Appendix 5

Internal Revenue Service (IRS) Forms

IRS Form SS-4 is used to apply for an Employer Identification Number (EIN) for the trust.

IRS Form 56 is the Notice Concerning Fiduciary Relationship. Trustees should file Form 56 to notify the IRS that they have become the trustee. Trustees who previously filed Form 56 and are resigning should file another Form 56 to notify the IRS that they are no longer the trustee.

IRS Form SS-4

Used to apply for Employer Identification Number (EIN) for the trust.

Form **SS-4** (Rev. January 2010) Department of the Treasury Internal Revenue Service

Application for Employer Identification Number

(For use by employers, corporations, partnerships, trusts, estates, churches, government agencies, Indian tribal entities, certain individuals, and others.)

► **See separate instructions for each line.** ► **Keep a copy for your records.**

OMB No. 1545-0003

EIN

Type or print clearly.

1 Legal name of entity (or individual) for whom the EIN is being requested

2 Trade name of business (if different from name on line 1)

3 Executor, administrator, trustee, "care of" name

4a Mailing address (room, apt., suite no. and street, or P.O. box)

5a Street address (if different) (Do not enter a P.O. box.)

4b City, state, and ZIP code (if foreign, see instructions)

5b City, state, and ZIP code (if foreign, see instructions)

6 County and state where principal business is located

7a Name of responsible party

7b SSN, ITIN, or EIN

8a Is this application for a limited liability company (LLC) (or a foreign equivalent)? . . . . ☐ **Yes** ☐ **No**

8b If 8a is "Yes," enter the number of LLC members . . . . ►

8c If 8a is "Yes," was the LLC organized in the United States? . . . . ☐ **Yes** ☐ **No**

9a **Type of entity** (check only one box). **Caution.** If 8a is "Yes," see the instructions for the correct box to check.

☐ Sole proprietor (SSN) ____
☐ Partnership
☐ Corporation (enter form number to be filed) ► ____
☐ Personal service corporation
☐ Church or church-controlled organization
☐ Other nonprofit organization (specify) ► ____
☐ Other (specify) ►

☐ Estate (SSN of decedent) ____
☐ Plan administrator (TIN) ____
☐ Trust (TIN of grantor) ____
☐ National Guard ☐ State/local government
☐ Farmers' cooperative ☐ Federal government/military
☐ REMIC ☐ Indian tribal governments/enterprises
Group Exemption Number (GEN) if any ►

9b If a corporation, name the state or foreign country (if applicable) where incorporated | State | Foreign country

10 **Reason for applying** (check only one box)

☐ Started new business (specify type) ► ____
☐ Hired employees (Check the box and see line 13.)
☐ Compliance with IRS withholding regulations
☐ Other (specify) ►

☐ Banking purpose (specify purpose) ► ____
☐ Changed type of organization (specify new type) ► ____
☐ Purchased going business
☐ Created a trust (specify type) ► ____
☐ Created a pension plan (specify type) ► ____

11 Date business started or acquired (month, day, year). See instructions.

12 Closing month of accounting year

13 Highest number of employees expected in the next 12 months (enter -0- if none). If no employees expected, skip line 14.

Agricultural	Household	Other

14 If you expect your employment tax liability to be $1,000 or less in a full calendar year **and** want to file Form 944 annually instead of Forms 941 quarterly, check here. (Your employment tax liability generally will be $1,000 or less if you expect to pay $4,000 or less in total wages.) If you do not check this box, you must file Form 941 for every quarter. ☐

15 First date wages or annuities were paid (month, day, year). **Note.** If applicant is a withholding agent, enter date income will first be paid to nonresident alien (month, day, year) . . . . ►

16 Check **one** box that best describes the principal activity of your business.
☐ Health care & social assistance ☐ Wholesale-agent/broker
☐ Construction ☐ Rental & leasing ☐ Transportation & warehousing ☐ Accommodation & food service ☐ Wholesale-other ☐ Retail
☐ Real estate ☐ Manufacturing ☐ Finance & insurance ☐ Other (specify)

17 Indicate principal line of merchandise sold, specific construction work done, products produced, or services provided.

18 Has the applicant entity shown on line 1 ever applied for and received an EIN? ☐ **Yes** ☐ **No**
If "Yes," write previous EIN here ►

Third Party Designee

Complete this section **only** if you want to authorize the named individual to receive the entity's EIN and answer questions about the completion of this form.

Designee's name — Designee's telephone number (include area code) ( )

Address and ZIP code — Designee's fax number (include area code) ( )

Under penalties of perjury, I declare that I have examined this application, and to the best of my knowledge and belief, it is true, correct, and complete.

Applicant's telephone number (include area code) ( )

Name and title (type or print clearly) ►

Applicant's fax number (include area code) ( )

Signature ► Date ►

For Privacy Act and Paperwork Reduction Act Notice, see separate instructions. Cat. No. 16055N Form **SS-4** (Rev. 1-2010)

Form SS-4 (Rev. 1-2010) Page **2**

Do I Need an EIN?

File Form SS-4 if the applicant entity does not already have an EIN but is required to show an EIN on any return, statement, or other document.[1] See also the separate instructions for each line on Form SS-4.

IF the applicant...	**AND...**	**THEN...**
Started a new business	Does not currently have (nor expect to have) employees	Complete lines 1, 2, 4a–8a, 8b–c (if applicable), 9a, 9b (if applicable), and 10–14 and 16–18.
Hired (or will hire) employees, including household employees	Does not already have an EIN	Complete lines 1, 2, 4a–6, 7a–b (if applicable), 8a, 8b–c (if applicable), 9a, 9b (if applicable), 10–18.
Opened a bank account	Needs an EIN for banking purposes only	Complete lines 1–5b, 7a–b (if applicable), 8a, 8b–c (if applicable), 9a, 9b (if applicable), 10, and 18.
Changed type of organization	Either the legal character of the organization or its ownership changed (for example, you incorporate a sole proprietorship or form a partnership) [2]	Complete lines 1–18 (as applicable).
Purchased a going business [3]	Does not already have an EIN	Complete lines 1–18 (as applicable).
Created a trust	The trust is other than a grantor trust or an IRA trust [4]	Complete lines 1–18 (as applicable).
Created a pension plan as a plan administrator [5]	Needs an EIN for reporting purposes	Complete lines 1, 3, 4a–5b, 9a, 10, and 18.
Is a foreign person needing an EIN to comply with IRS withholding regulations	Needs an EIN to complete a Form W-8 (other than Form W-8ECI), avoid withholding on portfolio assets, or claim tax treaty benefits [6]	Complete lines 1–5b, 7a–b (SSN or ITIN optional), 8a, 8b–c (if applicable), 9a, 9b (if applicable), 10, and 18.
Is administering an estate	Needs an EIN to report estate income on Form 1041	Complete lines 1–6, 9a, 10–12, 13–17 (if applicable), and 18.
Is a withholding agent for taxes on non-wage income paid to an alien (i.e., individual, corporation, or partnership, etc.)	Is an agent, broker, fiduciary, manager, tenant, or spouse who is required to file Form 1042, Annual Withholding Tax Return for U.S. Source Income of Foreign Persons	Complete lines 1, 2, 3 (if applicable), 4a–5b, 7a–b (if applicable), 8a, 8b–c (if applicable), 9a, 9b (if applicable), 10, and 18.
Is a state or local agency	Serves as a tax reporting agent for public assistance recipients under Rev. Proc. 80-4, 1980-1 C.B. 581 [7]	Complete lines 1, 2, 4a–5b, 9a, 10, and 18.
Is a single-member LLC	Needs an EIN to file Form 8832, Classification Election, for filing employment tax returns and excise tax returns, or for state reporting purposes [8]	Complete lines 1–18 (as applicable).
Is an S corporation	Needs an EIN to file Form 2553, Election by a Small Business Corporation [9]	Complete lines 1–18 (as applicable).

[1] For example, a sole proprietorship or self-employed farmer who establishes a qualified retirement plan, or is required to file excise, employment, alcohol, tobacco, or firearms returns, must have an EIN. A partnership, corporation, REMIC (real estate mortgage investment conduit), nonprofit organization (church, club, etc.), or farmers' cooperative must use an EIN for any tax-related purpose even if the entity does not have employees.

[2] However, do not apply for a new EIN if the existing entity only (a) changed its business name, (b) elected on Form 8832 to change the way it is taxed (or is covered by the default rules), or (c) terminated its partnership status because at least 50% of the total interests in partnership capital and profits were sold or exchanged within a 12-month period. The EIN of the terminated partnership should continue to be used. See Regulations section 301.6109-1(d)(2)(iii).

[3] Do not use the EIN of the prior business unless you became the "owner" of a corporation by acquiring its stock.

[4] However, grantor trusts that do not file using Optional Method 1 and IRA trusts that are required to file Form 990-T, Exempt Organization Business Income Tax Return, must have an EIN. For more information on grantor trusts, see the Instructions for Form 1041.

[5] A plan administrator is the person or group of persons specified as the administrator by the instrument under which the plan is operated.

[6] Entities applying to be a Qualified Intermediary (QI) need a QI-EIN even if they already have an EIN. See Rev. Proc. 2000-12.

[7] See also *Household employer* on page 4 of the instructions. **Note.** State or local agencies may need an EIN for other reasons, for example, hired employees.

[8] See *Disregarded entities* on page 4 of the instructions for details on completing Form SS-4 for an LLC.

[9] An existing corporation that is electing or revoking S corporation status should use its previously-assigned EIN.

IRS Form 56

Notice Concerning Fiduciary Relationship

Form **56**
(Rev. December 2007)
Department of the Treasury
Internal Revenue Service

Notice Concerning Fiduciary Relationship

(Internal Revenue Code sections 6036 and 6903)

OMB No. 1545-0013

Part I Identification

Name of person for whom you are acting (as shown on the tax return)	**Identifying number**	**Decedent's social security no.**
Address of person for whom you are acting (number, street, and room or suite no.)		
City or town, state, and ZIP code (If a foreign address, see instructions.)		
Fiduciary's name		
Address of fiduciary (number, street, and room or suite no.)		
City or town, state, and ZIP code	Telephone number (optional) ( )	

Part II Authority

1 Authority for fiduciary relationship. Check applicable box:

a(1) ☐ Will and codicils or court order appointing fiduciary . . . . **(2)** Date of death ....

b(1) ☐ Court order appointing fiduciary . . . . **(2)** Date (see instructions) ....

c ☐ Valid trust instrument and amendments

d ☐ Other. Describe ▶ ....

Part III Nature of Liability and Tax Notices

2 Type of tax (estate, gift, generation-skipping transfer, income, excise, etc.) ▶ ....

3 Federal tax form number (706, 1040, 1041, 1120, etc.) ▶ ....

4 Year(s) or period(s) (if estate tax, date of death) ▶ ....

5 If the fiduciary listed in Part I is the person to whom notices and other written communications should be sent for **all** items described on lines 2, 3, and 4, check here . . . . ▶ ☐

6 If the fiduciary listed in Part I is the person to whom notices and other written communications should be sent for **some** (but not all) of the items described on lines 2, 3, and 4, check here ▶ ☐ and list the applicable federal tax form number and the year(s) or period(s) applicable ....

....

Part IV Revocation or Termination of Notice

Section A—Total Revocation or Termination

7 Check this box if you are revoking or terminating all prior notices concerning fiduciary relationships on file with the Internal Revenue Service for the same tax matters and years or periods covered by this notice concerning fiduciary relationship . ▶ ☐

Reason for termination of fiduciary relationship. Check applicable box:

a ☐ Court order revoking fiduciary authority

b ☐ Certificate of dissolution or termination of a business entity

c ☐ Other. Describe ▶

Section B—Partial Revocation

8a Check this box if you are revoking earlier notices concerning fiduciary relationships on file with the Internal Revenue Service for the same tax matters and years or periods covered by this notice concerning fiduciary relationship . . . . ▶ ☐

b Specify to whom granted, date, and address, including ZIP code.

▶ ....

Section C—Substitute Fiduciary

9 Check this box if a new fiduciary or fiduciaries have been or will be substituted for the revoking or terminating fiduciary and specify the name(s) and address(es), including ZIP code(s), of the new fiduciary(ies) . . . . ▶ ☐

▶ ....

For Paperwork Reduction Act and Privacy Act Notice, see back page. Cat. No. 16375I Form **56** (Rev. 12-2007)

Form 56 (Rev. 12-2007) Page **2**

Part V **Court and Administrative Proceedings**

Name of court (if other than a court proceeding, identify the type of proceeding and name of agency)			Date proceeding initiated
Address of court			Docket number of proceeding
City or town, state, and ZIP code	Date	Time a.m. p.m.	Place of other proceedings

Part VI **Signature**

I certify that I have the authority to execute this notice concerning fiduciary relationship on behalf of the taxpayer.

Please Sign Here

Fiduciary's signature | Title, if applicable | Date

Form **56** (Rev. 12-2007)

Appendix 6

POMS SI 01120.203B1

The POMS (Program Operations Manual System) are guidelines that interpret the Social Security laws. POMS SI 01120.203, which updates an earlier version of the POMS, was enacted in January 2009. Section B1f applies to initial bank accounts for self-funded special needs trusts.

TN 40 (01-09)

SI 01120.203 Exceptions to Counting Trusts Established on or after 1/1/00

Topic	Reference
Introduction to Medicaid Trust Exceptions	SI 01120.203A
Policy—Exception To Counting Medicaid Trusts	SI 01120.203B
Policy—Waiver For Undue Hardship	SI 01120.203C
Procedure— Developing Exceptions To Resource Counting	SI 01120.203D
Procedure—Development Of Undue Hardship Waiver	SI 01120.203E
Procedure—Nonprofit Associations	SI 01120.203F
Procedure—Follow-Up To A Finding Of Undue Hardship	SI 01120.203G
Procedure—Reevaluating Revocable Trusts Processed Under The Policy In Effect From 1/1/2000 Through 1/31/2001	SI 01120.203H

A. Introduction to Medicaid Trust Exceptions

We refer to the exceptions discussed in this section as **Medicaid trust exceptions** because sections 1917(d)(4)(A) and (C) of the Social Security Act (the Act) (42 U.S.C. § 1396p(d)(4)(A) and (C)) set forth exceptions to the general rule of counting trusts as income and resources for the purposes of Medicaid eligibility and can be found in the Medicaid provisions of the Act. While these exceptions are also Supplemental Security Income (SSI) exceptions, we refer to them as Medicaid trust exceptions to distinguish them from other exceptions to counting trusts provided in the SSI law (e.g., undue hardship) and because the term has become a term of common usage.

Development and evaluation of Medicaid trust exceptions are based on the type of trust under review. There are two types of Medicaid trusts to consider:

- Special Needs Trusts
- Pooled Trusts

B. Policy—Exception To Counting Medicaid Trusts

1. Special Needs Trusts Established under Section 1917(d)(4)(A) of the Act

a. General -- Special Needs Trusts

NOTE: Although this exception is commonly referred to as the **special needs** trust exception, the exception applies to any trust meeting the following requirements and does not have to be a strict **special needs** trust.

The resource counting provisions of Section 1613(e) do not apply to a trust:

- Which contains the assets of an individual **under age 65** and who is **disabled**; and
- Which is **established for the benefit of such individual through the actions of a parent, grandparent, legal guardian or a court**; and
- Which provides that the **State(s) will receive all amounts remaining** in the trust upon the death of the individual up to an amount equal to the total medical assistance paid on behalf of the individual under a State Medicaid plan.

CAUTION: A trust which meets the exception to counting the trust under the SSI statutory trust provisions of Section 1613(e) must still be evaluated under the instructions in SI 01120.200 to determine if it is a countable resource. If the trust meets the definition of a resource (SI 01110.100B.1.), it would will be subject to regular resource-counting rules.

b. Under Age 65

To qualify for the special needs trust exception, the trust must be established for the benefit of a disabled individual under age 65. This exception does not apply to a trust established for the benefit of an individual age 65 or older. If the trust was established for the benefit of a disabled individual prior to the date the individual attained age 65, the exception continues to apply after the individual reaches age 65.

c. Additions to Trust After Age 65

Additions to or augmentation of a trust after age 65 (except as outlined below) are not subject to this exception. Such additions may be income in the month added to the trust, depending on the source of the funds (see SI 01120.201J.) and may be counted as resources in the following months under regular SSI trust rules.

Additions or augmentation do not include interest, dividends or other earnings of the trust or portion of the trust meeting the special needs trust exception. If the trust contains the irrevocable assignment of the right to receive payments from an annuity or support payments made when the trust beneficiary was less than 65 years of age, annuity or support payments paid to a special needs trust are treated the same as payments made before the individual attained age 65 and do not disqualify the trust from the special needs trust exception.

d. Disabled

To qualify for the special needs trust exception, the individual whose assets were used to establish the trust must be disabled for SSI purposes under section 1614(a)(3) of the Act.

e. Established for the Benefit of the Individual

Under the special needs trust exception, the trust must be established for and used for the benefit of the disabled individual. SSA has interpreted this provision to require that the trust be for the sole benefit of the individual, as described in SI 01120.201F.2. Any provisions that:

- provide benefits to other individuals or entities during the disabled individual's lifetime, or
- allow for termination of the trust prior to the individual's death and payment of the corpus to another individual or entity (other than the State(s) or another creditor for payment for goods or services provided to the individual), will result in

disqualification for the special needs trust exception.

Payments to third parties for goods and services provided to the trust beneficiary are allowed. However, such payments should be evaluated under POMS SI 01120.200E. - SI 01120.200F. and SI 01120.201I. to determine whether the payments may be income to the individual.

f. Who Established the Trust

The special needs trust exception does not apply to a trust established through the actions of the disabled individual himself/herself. To qualify for the special needs trust exception, the assets of the disabled individual must be put into a trust established through the actions of the disabled individual's:

- parent(s);
- grandparent(s);
- legal guardian(s); or
- a court.

In the case of a legally competent, disabled adult, a parent or grandparent may establish a "seed" trust using a nominal amount of his or her own money, or if State law allows, an empty or dry trust. After the seed trust is established, the legally competent disabled adult may transfer his or her own assets to the trust or another individual with legal authority (e.g. power of attorney) may transfer the individual's assets into the trust.

In the case of a trust established through the actions of a court, the creation of the trust must be required by a court order. Approval of a trust by a court is not sufficient.

NOTE: Under 1613(e) of the Act, a trust is considered to have been "established by" an individual if any of the individual's (or the individual's spouse) assets are transferred to the trust other by will. Alternatively, under the Medicaid trust exceptions in 1917(d)(4)(A) and (C) of the Act, a trust can be "established by" an individual who does not provide the corpus of the trust, or transfer any of his/her assets to the trust, but rather someone who took action to establish the trust. To avoid confusion, we use the phrase "established through the actions of" rather than "established by" when referring to the individual who physically took action to establish a special needs or pooled trust.

g. Legal Authority and Trusts

The person establishing the trust with the assets of the individual or transferring the assets of the individual to the trust must have legal authority to act with respect to the assets of that individual. Attempting to establish a trust with the assets of another individual without proper legal authority to act with respect to the assets of the individual will generally result in an invalid trust.

For example, a parent establishing a seed trust for his adult child with his own assets has legal authority over his own assets to establish a trust. He only needs legal authority over his child's assets if he actually takes action with the child's assets, e.g., transfers them to a previously established trust.

A power of attorney (POA) is legal authority to act with respect to the assets of a disabled individual. However, a trust established under a POA will result in a trust we consider to be established through the actions of the disabled individual himself/herself because the POA merely establishes an agency relationship.

h. State Medicaid Reimbursement Requirement

To qualify for the special needs trust exception, the trust must contain specific language that provides that upon the death of the individual, the State(s) will receive all amounts remaining in the trust, up to an amount equal to the total amount of medical assistance paid on behalf of the individual under the State Medicaid plan(s). The State(s) must be listed as the first payee and have priority over payment of other debts and administrative expenses except as listed in SI 01120.203B.3.a.

The trust must provide payback for any State(s) that may have provided medical assistance under the State Medicaid plan(s) and not be limited to any particular State(s). Medicaid payback may also not be limited to any particular period of time, i.e. payback cannot be limited to the period after establishment of the trust.

NOTE: Labeling the trust as a **Medicaid pay-back trust**, **OBRA 1993 pay-back trust**, trust **established in accordance with 42 U.S.C. § 1396p**, or as an **MQT**, etc. is not sufficient to meet the requirements for this exception. The trust must contain language substantially similar to the language above. An oral trust cannot meet this requirement.

2. Pooled Trusts Established under Section 1917(d)(4)(C) of the Act

a. General – Pooled Trusts

A pooled trust is a trust established and administered by an organization. It is sometimes called a "master trust" because it contains the assets of many different individuals, each in separate accounts established through the actions of individuals, and each with a beneficiary. By analogy, the pooled trust is like a bank that holds the assets of individual account holders.

Whenever you are evaluating the trust, it is important to distinguish between the master trust, which is established through the actions of the nonprofit association, and the individual trust accounts within the master trust, which are established through the actions of the individual or another person for the individual.

The provisions of the SSI trust statute do not apply to a trust containing the **assets of a disabled individual** which meets the following conditions:

- The pooled trust is established and maintained by a **nonprofit association**;
- **Separate accounts** are maintained for each beneficiary, but assets are pooled for investing and management purposes;
- Accounts **are established solely for the benefit of the disabled individuals;**
- The account in the trust is **established through the actions of the individual, a parent, grandparent, legal guardian, or a court**; and
- The trust provides that to the extent any amounts remaining in the beneficiary's account upon the death of the beneficiary are not retained by the trust, **the trust will pay to the State(s)** the amount remaining up to an amount equal to the total amount of medical assistance paid on behalf of the beneficiary under State Medicaid plan(s).

NOTE: There is no age restriction under this exception. However, a transfer of resources to a trust for an individual age 65 or over may result in a transfer penalty (see SI 01150.121.).

CAUTION: A trust which meets the exception to counting the trust under the SSI statutory trust provisions of 1613(e) must still be evaluated under the instructions in SI 01120.200 to determine if it is a countable resource.

Appendix 7

Federal Housing Income and Asset Rules

Tenants in public housing programs pay rent based on a percentage of their income. The income rules are listed in 24 CFR § 5.609. (CFR stands for the Code of Federal Regulations.) There is no asset limit for federal public housing. However, in some cases, earnings generated by an asset are considered to be income that will increase the person's rent. The rules on assets (including trusts) are located at 24 CFR § 5.603.

24 CFR § 5.603

Definition of Assets used by Federal Housing Programs

[Code of Federal Regulations]
[Title 24, Volume 1]
[Revised as of April 1, 2008]
From the U.S. Government Printing Office via GPO Access
[CITE: 24CFR5.603]

[Page 78-80]

TITLE 24--HOUSING AND URBAN DEVELOPMENT

PART 5_GENERAL HUD PROGRAM REQUIREMENTS; WAIVERS--Table of Contents

Subpart F_Section 8 and Public Housing, and Other HUD Assisted Housing

Sec. 5.603 Definitions.

As used in this subpart:

(a) Terms found elsewhere in part 5--(1) Subpart A. The terms 1937 Act, elderly person, public housing, public housing agency (PHA), responsible entity and Section 8 are defined in Sec. 5.100.

(2) Subpart D. The terms "disabled family", "elderly family", "family", "live-in aide", and "person with disabilities" are defined in Sec. 5.403.

(b) The following terms shall have the meanings set forth below:

Adjusted income. See Sec. 5.611.

Annual income. See Sec. 5.609.

Child care expenses. Amounts anticipated to be paid by the family for the care of children under 13 years of age during the period for which annual income is computed, but only where such care is necessary to enable a family member to actively seek employment, be gainfully employed, or to further his or her education and only to the extent such amounts are not reimbursed. The amount deducted shall reflect reasonable charges for child care. In the case of child care necessary to permit employment, the amount deducted shall not exceed the amount of employment income that is included in annual income.

Dependent. A member of the family (except foster children and foster adults) other than the family head or spouse, who is under 18 years of age, or is a person with a disability, or is a full-time student.

Disability assistance expenses. Reasonable expenses that are anticipated, during the period for which annual income is computed, for attendant care and auxiliary apparatus for a disabled family member and that are necessary to enable a family member (including the disabled member) to be employed, provided that the expenses are neither paid to a member of the family nor reimbursed by an outside source.

Economic self-sufficiency program. Any program designed to encourage, assist, train, or facilitate the economic independence of HUD-assisted families or to provide work for such families. These programs include programs for job training, employment counseling, work placement, basic skills training, education, English proficiency, workfare, financial or household management, apprenticeship, and any program necessary to ready a participant for work (including a substance abuse or mental health treatment program), or other work activities.

Extremely low income family. A family whose annual income does not exceed 30 percent of the median income for the area, as determined by HUD, with adjustments for smaller and larger families, except that HUD may establish income ceilings higher or lower than 30 percent of the median income for the area if HUD finds that such variations are necessary because of unusually high or low family incomes.

Full-time student. A person who is attending school or vocational training on a full-time basis.

Imputed welfare income. See Sec. 5.615.

Low income family. A family whose annual income does not exceed 80 percent of the median income for the area, as determined by HUD with adjustments for smaller and larger families, except that HUD may establish income ceilings higher or lower than 80 percent of the median income for the area on the basis of HUD's findings that such variations are necessary because of unusually high or low family incomes.

Medical expenses. Medical expenses, including medical insurance premiums, that are anticipated during the period for which annual income is computed, and that are not covered by insurance.

Monthly adjusted income. One twelfth of adjusted income.

Monthly income. One twelfth of annual income.

Net family assets. (1) Net cash value after deducting reasonable costs that would be incurred in disposing of real property, savings, stocks, bonds, and other forms of capital investment, excluding interests in Indian trust land and excluding equity accounts in HUD homeownership programs. The value of necessary items of personal property such as furniture and automobiles shall be excluded.

(2) In cases where a trust fund has been established and the trust is not revocable by, or under the control of, any member of the family or household, the value of the trust fund will not be considered an asset so long as the fund continues to be held in trust. Any income distributed from the trust fund shall be counted when determining annual income under Sec. 5.609.

(3) In determining net family assets, PHAs or owners, as applicable, shall include the value of any business or family assets disposed of by an applicant or tenant for less than fair market value (including a disposition in trust, but not in a foreclosure or bankruptcy sale) during the two years preceding the date of application for the program or reexamination, as applicable, in excess of the consideration received therefor. In the case of a disposition as part of a separation or divorce settlement, the disposition will not be considered to be for less than fair market value if the applicant or tenant receives important consideration not measurable in dollar terms.

(4) For purposes of determining annual income under Sec. 5.609, the term "net family assets" does not include the value of a home currently being purchased with assistance under part 982, subpart M of this title. This exclusion is limited to the first 10 years after the purchase date of the home.

Owner has the meaning provided in the relevant program regulations. As used in this subpart, where appropriate, the term "owner" shall also include a "borrower" as defined in part 891 of this title.

Responsible entity. For Sec. 5.611, in addition to the definition of "responsible entity" in Sec. 5.100, and for Sec. 5.617, in addition to only that part of the definition of "responsible entity" in Sec. 5.100 which addresses the Section 8 program covered by Sec. 5.617 (public housing is not covered by Sec. 5.617), "responsible entity" means:

(1) For the HOME Investment Partnerships Program, the participating jurisdiction, as defined in 24 CFR 92.2;

(2) For the Rent Supplement Payments Program, the owner of the multifamily project;

(3) For the Rental Assistance Payments Program, the owner of the Section 236 project;

(4) For the Housing Opportunities for Persons with AIDS (HOPWA) program, the applicable "State" or "unit of general local government" or "nonprofit organization" as these terms are defined in 24 CFR 574.3, that administers the HOPWA Program;

(5) For the Shelter Plus Care Program, the "Recipient" as defined in 24 CFR 582.5;

(6) For the Supportive Housing Program, the "recipient" as defined in 24 CFR 583.5;

(7) For the Section 202 Supportive Housing Program for the Elderly, the "Owner" as defined in 24 CFR 891.205;

(8) For the Section 202 Direct Loans for Housing for the Elderly and Persons with Disabilities), the "Borrower'" as defined in 24 CFR 891.505; and

(9) For the Section 811 Supportive Housing Program for Persons with Disabilities, the "owner" as defined in 24 CFR 891.305

Tenant rent. The amount payable monthly by the family as rent to the unit owner (Section 8 owner or PHA in public housing). (This term is not used in the Section 8 voucher program.)

Total tenant payment. See Sec. 5.613.

Utility allowance. If the cost of utilities (except telephone) and other housing services for an assisted unit is not included in the tenant rent but is the responsibility of the family occupying the unit, an amount equal to the estimate made or approved by a PHA or HUD of the monthly cost of a reasonable consumption of such utilities and other services for the unit by an energy-conservative household of modest circumstances consistent with the requirements of a safe, sanitary, and healthful living environment.

Utility reimbursement. The amount, if any, by which the utility allowance for a unit, if applicable, exceeds the total tenant payment for the family occupying the unit. (This definition is not used in the Section 8 voucher program, or for a public housing family that is paying a flat rent.)

Very low income family. A family whose annual income does not exceed 50 percent of the median family income for the area, as determined by HUD with adjustments for smaller and larger families, except that HUD may establish income ceilings higher or lower than 50 percent of the median income for the area if HUD finds that such variations are necessary because of unusually high or low family incomes.

Welfare assistance. Welfare or other payments to families or individuals, based on need, that are made under programs funded, separately or jointly, by Federal, State or local governments (including assistance provided under the Temporary Assistance for Needy Families (TANF) program, as that term is defined under the implementing regulations issued by the Department of Health and Human Services at 45 CFR 260.31).

Work activities. See definition at section 407(d) of the Social Security Act (42 U.S.C. 607(d)).

[61 FR 54498, Oct. 18, 1996, as amended at 65 FR 16716, Mar. 29, 2000; 65 FR 55161, Sept. 12, 2000; 66 FR 6223, Jan. 19, 2001; 67 FR 47432, July 18, 2002]

24 CFR § 5.609

Definition of Assets used by Federal Housing Programs

[Code of Federal Regulations]
[Title 24, Volume 1]
[Revised as of April 1, 2008]
From the U.S. Government Printing Office via GPO Access
[CITE: 24CFR5.609]

[Page 80-83]

TITLE 24--HOUSING AND URBAN DEVELOPMENT

PART 5_GENERAL HUD PROGRAM REQUIREMENTS; WAIVERS--Table of Contents

Subpart F_Section 8 and Public Housing, and Other HUD Assisted Housing

Sec. 5.609 Annual income.

(a) Annual income means all amounts, monetary or not, which:

(1) Go to, or on behalf of, the family head or spouse (even if temporarily absent) or to any other family member; or

(2) Are anticipated to be received from a source outside the family during the 12-month period following admission or annual reexamination effective date; and

(3) Which are not specifically excluded in paragraph (c) of this section.

(4) Annual income also means amounts derived (during the 12-month period) from assets to which any member of the family has access.

(b) Annual income includes, but is not limited to:

(1) The full amount, before any payroll deductions, of wages and salaries, overtime pay, commissions, fees, tips and bonuses, and other

compensation for personal services;

(2) The net income from the operation of a business or profession. Expenditures for business expansion or amortization of capital indebtedness shall not be used as deductions in determining net income. An allowance for depreciation of assets used in a business or profession may be deducted, based on straight line depreciation, as provided in Internal Revenue Service regulations. Any withdrawal of cash or assets from the operation of a business or profession will be included in income, except to the extent the withdrawal is reimbursement of cash or assets invested in the operation by the family;

(3) Interest, dividends, and other net income of any kind from real or personal property. Expenditures for amortization of capital indebtedness shall not be used as deductions in determining net income. An allowance for depreciation is permitted only as authorized in paragraph (b)(2) of this section. Any withdrawal of cash or assets from an investment will be included in income, except to the extent the withdrawal is reimbursement of cash or assets invested by the family. Where the family has net family assets in excess of $5,000, annual income shall include the greater of the actual income derived from all net family assets or a percentage of the value of such assets based on the current passbook savings rate, as determined by HUD;

(4) The full amount of periodic amounts received from Social Security, annuities, insurance policies, retirement funds, pensions, disability or death benefits, and other similar types of periodic receipts, including a lump-sum amount or prospective monthly amounts for the delayed start of a periodic amount (except as provided in paragraph (c)(14) of this section);

(5) Payments in lieu of earnings, such as unemployment and disability compensation, worker's compensation and severance pay (except as provided in paragraph (c)(3) of this section); (6) Welfare assistance payments. (i) Welfare assistance payments made under the Temporary Assistance for Needy Families (TANF) program are included in annual income only to the extent such payments:

(A) Qualify as assistance under the TANF program definition at 45 CFR 260.31; and

(B) Are not otherwise excluded under paragraph (c) of this section.

(ii) If the welfare assistance payment includes an amount specifically designated for shelter and utilities that is subject to adjustment by the welfare assistance agency in accordance with the actual cost of shelter and utilities, the amount of welfare assistance income to be included as income shall consist of:

(A) The amount of the allowance or grant exclusive of the amount specifically designated for shelter or utilities; plus

(B) The maximum amount that the welfare assistance agency could in fact allow the family for shelter and utilities. If the family's welfare assistance is ratably reduced from the standard of need by applying a percentage, the amount calculated under this paragraph shall be the amount resulting from one application of the percentage.

(7) Periodic and determinable allowances, such as alimony and child support payments, and regular contributions or gifts received from organizations or from persons not residing in the dwelling;

(8) All regular pay, special pay and allowances of a member of the Armed Forces (except as provided in paragraph (c)(7) of this section).

(9) For Section 8 programs only and as provided in 24 CFR 5.612, any financial assistance, in excess of amounts received for tuition, that an individual receives under the Higher Education Act of 1965 (20 U.S.C. 1001 et seq.), from private sources, or from an institution of higher education (as defined under the Higher Education Act of 1965 (20 U.S.C. 1002)), shall be considered income to that individual, except that financial assistance described in this paragraph is not considered annual income for persons over the age of 23 with dependent children. For purposes of this paragraph, "financial assistance" does not include loan proceeds for the purpose of determining income.

(c) Annual income does not include the following:

(1) Income from employment of children (including foster children) under the age of 18 years;

(2) Payments received for the care of foster children or foster adults (usually persons with disabilities, unrelated to the tenant family, who are unable to live alone);

(3) Lump-sum additions to family assets, such as inheritances, insurance payments (including payments under health and accident insurance and worker's compensation), capital gains and settlement for

personal or property losses (except as provided in paragraph (b)(5) of this section);

(4) Amounts received by the family that are specifically for, or in reimbursement of, the cost of medical expenses for any family member;

(5) Income of a live-in aide, as defined in Sec. 5.403;

(6) Subject to paragraph (b)(9) of this section, the full amount of student financial assistance paid directly to the student or to the educational institution;

(7) The special pay to a family member serving in the Armed Forces who is exposed to hostile fire;

(8)(i) Amounts received under training programs funded by HUD;

(ii) Amounts received by a person with a disability that are disregarded for a limited time for purposes of Supplemental Security Income eligibility and benefits because they are set aside for use under a Plan to Attain Self-Sufficiency (PASS);

(iii) Amounts received by a participant in other publicly assisted programs which are specifically for or in reimbursement of out-of-pocket expenses incurred (special equipment, clothing, transportation, child care, etc.) and which are made solely to allow participation in a specific program;

(iv) Amounts received under a resident service stipend. A resident service stipend is a modest amount (not to exceed $200 per month) received by a resident for performing a service for the PHA or owner, on a part-time basis, that enhances the quality of life in the development. Such services may include, but are not limited to, fire patrol, hall monitoring, lawn maintenance, resident initiatives coordination, and serving as a member of the PHA's governing board. No resident may receive more than one such stipend during the same period of time;

(v) Incremental earnings and benefits resulting to any family member from participation in qualifying State or local employment training programs (including training programs not affiliated with a local government) and training of a family member as resident management staff. Amounts excluded by this provision must be received under employment training programs with clearly defined goals and objectives, and are excluded only for the period during which the family member participates in the employment training program;

(9) Temporary, nonrecurring or sporadic income (including gifts);

(10) Reparation payments paid by a foreign government pursuant to claims filed under the laws of that government by persons who were persecuted during the Nazi era;

(11) Earnings in excess of $480 for each full-time student 18 years old or older (excluding the head of household and spouse);

(12) Adoption assistance payments in excess of $480 per adopted child;

(13) [Reserved]

(14) Deferred periodic amounts from supplemental security income and social security benefits that are received in a lump sum amount or in prospective monthly amounts.

(15) Amounts received by the family in the form of refunds or rebates under State or local law for property taxes paid on the dwelling unit;

(16) Amounts paid by a State agency to a family with a member who has a developmental disability and is living at home to offset the cost of services and equipment needed to keep the developmentally disabled family member at home; or

(17) Amounts specifically excluded by any other Federal statute from consideration as income for purposes of determining eligibility or benefits under a category of assistance programs that includes assistance under any program to which the exclusions set forth in 24 CFR 5.609(c) apply. A notice will be published in the Federal Register and distributed to PHAs and housing owners identifying the benefits that qualify for this exclusion. Updates will be published and distributed when necessary.

(d) Annualization of income. If it is not feasible to anticipate a level of income over a 12-month period (e.g., seasonal or cyclic income), or the PHA believes that past income is the best available indicator of expected future income, the PHA may annualize the income anticipated for a shorter period, subject to a redetermination at the end of the shorter period.

[61 FR 54498, Oct, 18, 1996, as amended at 65 FR 16716, Mar. 29, 2000; 67 FR 47432, July 18, 2002; 70 FR 77743, Dec. 30, 2005]

Index

A

B

C

D

E

F

L

M

N

O

P

Q

R

S

T

U

V

W